Aliens, Gods,

and Other

Paranormal

Native American Indian Tales

Written and Edited by G.W. Mullins
With Original Art by C.L. Hause

Light Of The Moon Publishing

ISBN: 978-1-958221-05-1

First Edition Printing

Light Of The Moon Publishing has allowed this work to remain exactly as the author intended, verbatim, without editorial input.

Printed in the United States of America

The following book represents a collection of Native American works which are public domain. You may have read the stories before. In true story telling fashion, the stories have been left as close to the original form as possible. In Native American culture, in order to pass the stories along with all information intact, they had to be told pretty much word for word, to keep the legends alive. Many of these stories were translated directly from original Native language texts. With that in mind, please be aware that some spellings and word usage may vary from one tribe to another. For instance, the spelling of "teepee", as used in this book, can also be written as "tipi", and "tepee". All are correct. Also, when using words like "someone", in most native cultures, it would be "some one". So, keep in mind, these are not necessarily misspellings. They are simply dialect and translations.

This book is dedicated to Vince Mullins, my Grandfather (Pawpaw). He was a tall red man with fire in his eyes... who I loved so much.

This book is also dedicated to one of my heroes, Chief Dan George, a true visionary.

G.W. Mullins

Chief Dan George, (July 24, 1899 – September 23, 1981) was a chief of the Tsleil-Waututh Nation, a Coast Salish band located on Burrard Inlet in North Vancouver, British Columbia, Canada. He was also an author, poet, actor, and an Officer of the Order of Canada. At the age of 71, he was nominated for an Academy Award for Best Supporting Actor in Little Big Man.

You have noticed that everything as Indian does is in a circle, and that is because the Power of the World always works in circles, and everything tries to be round.... The Sky is round, and I have heard that the earth is round like a ball, and so are all the stars. The wind, in its greatest power, whirls. Birds make their nest in circles, for theirs is the same religion as ours....

~Black Elk, Oglala Sioux Holy Man, 1863-1950

Also Available From G.W. Mullins And C.L. Hause

Star People, Sky Gods And Other Tales Of The Native American Indians

Coyote Tales Of The Native American Indians

Bear Tales Of The Native American Indians

More Star People, Sky Gods And Other Paranormal Tales Of The Native American Indians

Walking With Spirits Native American Myths, Legends, And Folklore Volumes One Thru Six

The Native American Cookbook

Native American Cooking - An Indian Cookbook With Legends And Folklore

The Native American Story Book - Stories Of The American Indians For Children Volumes One Thru Five

The Best Native American Stories For Children

Cherokee A Collection of American Indian Legends, Stories And Fables

Creation Myths - Tales Of The Native American Indians

Strange Tales Of The Native American Indians

Spirit Quest - Stories Of The Native American Indians

Animal Tales Of The Native American Indians

Medicine Man - Shamanism, Natural Healing, Remedies And Stories Of The Native American Indians

Native American Legends: Stories Of The Hopi Indians Volumes 1 and 2

Totem Animals Of The Native Americans

The Best Native American Myths, Legends And Folklore Volumes 1 Thru 3

Ghosts, Spirits And The Afterlife In Native American Indian Mythology And Folklore

The Native American Art Book – Art Inspired By Native American Myths And Legends

Animal Tales Of The native American Indians Vol. 2

Origin Tales Of The Native American Indians

This is the Earth, healed again, growing green and blue.
I want you to remember this exactly as it is,
and then go and tell the people that if enough of us hold this
image in their minds,
we can heal the Earth and make it like it was a long time ago.

- Grandfather Rolling Thunder, Cherokee Medicine Elder

Lakota Instructions for Living

Friend do it this way - that is,
whatever you do in life,
do the very best you can
with both your heart and mind.

And if you do it that way,
the Power Of The Universe
will come to your assistance,
if your heart and mind are in Unity.

When one sits in the Hoop Of The People,
one must be responsible because
All of Creation is related.
And the hurt of one is the hurt of all.
And the honor of one is the honor of all.
And whatever we do affects everything in the
universe.

If you do it that way - that is,
if you truly join your heart and mind
as One - whatever you ask for,
that's the Way It's Going To Be.

Passed down from White Buffalo Calf Woman

Table of Contents

Introduction

Native American Mythology began long before the
European settlers arrived on North American soil.
Contrary to popular beliefs, there is more to Native
American Folklore than stories of buffalo hunts, teepee
living and animal stories. Hundreds of tribes throughout
North American created a huge mythological system that
has rivaled that of the Greeks. Many of these tales have
been lost, or are often hard to find. This collection
represents a history that should be remembered.

As a Native American myself, I embrace these stories.
Native Americans tribes offer such a rich heritage. They
have recorded a huge amount of their history through
storytelling. In these stories you will relive their history
and the lives of North America's First People.

The stories in this book have been handed down from
generation to generation. And in such tradition, they are
now handed down to you, to share with the next generation.

Included in this anthology, are a group of collected works
from the well-known, to the often-forgotten tribes. The
tales included within this book, feature some of the most
familiar and popular recorded… Gods, Aliens and all
things Paranormal.

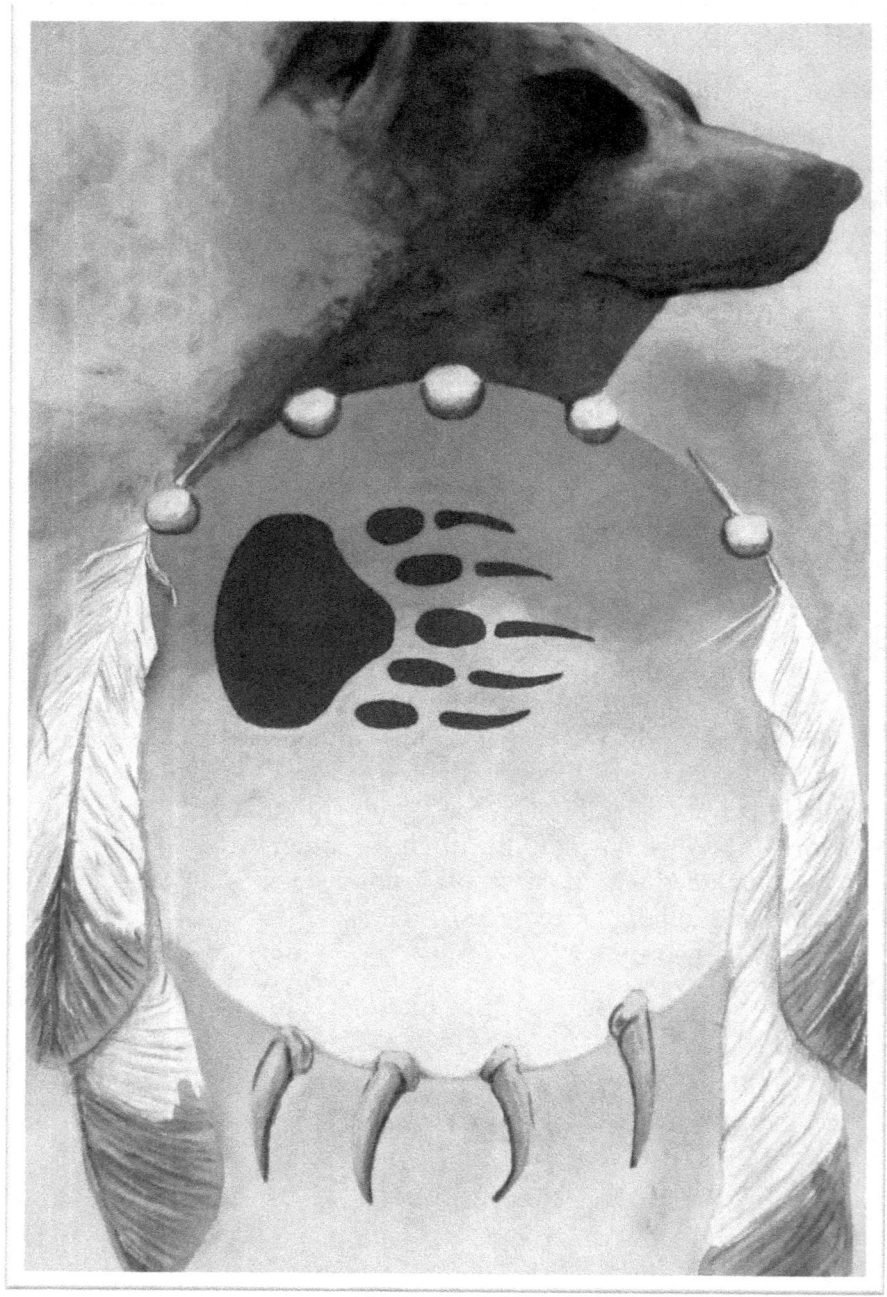

The Star Feathers

Cherokee

A long time ago a warrior of roving disposition went down into the white settlements toward the east, where for the first time he saw a peacock. The beautiful long feathers surprised and delighted him, and by trading some valuable Indian possession of his own he managed to buy a few of them, which he took with him to the mountains and hid, until he was ready to use them, in an old beaver lodge under the river bank. To get into the beaver lodge he had to dive under the water.

Then he set to work secretly and made himself a headdress, with the long peacock feathers in the front and trailing out behind and the shorter ones at the sides. At the next dance he wore the new headdress, and asserted that he had been up to the sky and that these were star feathers (see number 9, "What the stars are like"). He made a long speech also, which he pretended was a message he had received from the star spirits to deliver to the people.

Everyone wondered at the beautiful feathers, so different from any they had ever seen before. They made no doubt that he had been up to the sky and talked with spirits. He became a great prophet, and used to keep himself hidden all day in the beaver hole, and whenever there was a night gathering for a dance or a council, he would suddenly appear among them wearing his feather headdress and give the people a new message from the sky. Then he would leave them again, pretending that he went up to heaven.

He grew famous, and powerful among all the medicine men, until at last it happened that another Cherokee went down among the white settlements and saw there another peacock, and knew at once that the prophet was a fraud. On his return he quietly told some of his friends, and they decided to investigate. When the next night dance came around the prophet was on hand as usual with a new message fresh from the stars. The people listened reverently, and promised to do all that he commanded. Then he left them, saying that he must return at once to the sky, but as he went out from the circle the spies followed him in the darkness, and saw him go down to the river and dive under the water. They waited, but he, did not come up again, and they went back and told the people. The next morning a party went to the spot and discovered the beaver lodge under the bank. One man dived and came up inside, and there he found the prophet sitting with the peacock feathers by his side.

The Nûñnë'hï And Other Spirit Folk

Cherokee

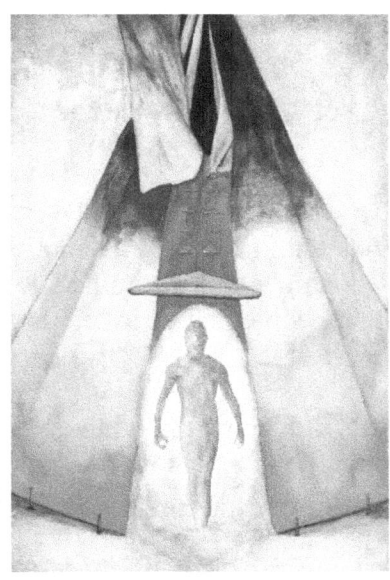

The *Nûñnë'hï* or immortals, the "people who live anywhere," were a race of spirit people who lived in the highlands of the old Cherokee country and had a great many townhouses, especially in the bald mountains, the high peaks on which no timber ever grows.

They had large townhouses in Pilot knob and under the old Nïkwäsï' mound in North Carolina, and another under Blood Mountain, at the head of Nottely river, in Georgia. They were invisible excepting when they wanted to be seen, and then they looked and poke just like other Indians. They were very fond of music and dancing, and hunters in the mountains would often hear the dance, songs and the drum beating in some invisible townhouse, but when they went toward the sound it would shift about and they would hear it behind them or away in some other direction, so that they could never find the place where the dance was.

They were a friendly people, too, and often brought lost wanderers to their townhouses under the mountains and cared for them there until they were rested and then guided them back to their home. More than once, also, when the Cherokee were hard pressed by the enemy, the Nûñnë'hï warriors have come out, as they did at old Nïkwäsï', and have saved them from defeat. Some people have thought that they are the same as the Yûñwï Tsunsdi', the "Little People"; but these are fairies, no larger in size than children.

There was a man in Nottely town who had been with the Nûñnë'hï when he was a boy, and he told Wafford all about it. He was a truthful, hard-headed man, and Wafford had heard the story so often from other people that he asked this man to tell it. It was in this way:

When he was about 10 or 12 years old, he was playing one day near the river, shooting at a mark with his how and arrows, until he became tired, and started to build a fish trap in the water. While he was piling up the stones in two long walls a man came and stood on the bank and asked him what he was doing. The boy told him, and the man said, "Well, that's pretty hard work and you ought to rest a while. Come and take a walk up the river." The boy said, "No"; that he was going home to dinner soon. "Come right up to my house," said the stranger, and I'll give you a good dinner there and bring you home again in the morning."

So, the boy went with him up the river until they came to a house, when they went in, and the man's wife and the other people there were very glad to see him, and gave him a fine dinner, and were very kind to him. While they were eating a man that the boy knew very well came in and spoke to him, so that he felt quite at home.

After dinner he played with the other children and slept there that night, and in the morning, after breakfast, the man got ready to take him home. They went down a path that had a cornfield on one side and a peach orchard fenced in on the other, until they came to another trail, and the man said, "Go along this trail across that ridge and you will come to the river road that will bring you straight to your home, and now I'll go back to the house." So, the man went back to the house and the boy went on along the trail, but when he had gone a little way he looked back, and there was no cornfield or orchard or fence or house; nothing but trees on the mountain side.

He thought it very queer, but somehow, he was not frightened, and went on until he came to the river trail in sight of his home. There were a great many people standing about talking, and when they saw him, they ran toward him shouting, "Here he is! He is not drowned or killed in the mountains!" They told him they had been hunting him ever since yesterday noon, and asked him where he had been.

"A man took me over to his house just across the ridge, and I had a fine dinner and a good time with the children," said the boy, "I thought Udsi'skalä here"--that was the name of the man he had seen at dinner--"would tell you where I was." But Udsi'skalä said, "I haven't seen you. I was out all day in my canoe hunting you. It was one of the Nûñnë'hï that made himself look like me."

Then his mother said, "You say you had dinner there?" "Yes, and I had plenty, too," said the boy; but his mother answered, "There is no house there--only trees and rocks-- but we hear a drum sometimes in the big bald above. The people you saw were the Nûñnë'hï."

Once four Nûñnë'hï women came, to a dance at Nottely town, and danced half the night with the young men there, and nobody knew that they were Nûñnë'hï, but thought them visitors from another settlement. About midnight they left to go home, and some men who had come out from the townhouse to cool off watched to see which way they went.

They saw the women go down the trail to the river ford, but just as they came to the water they disappeared, although it was a plain trail, with no place where they could hide. Then the watchers knew they were Nûñnë'hï women. Several men saw this happen, and one of them was Wafford's father-in-law, who was known for an honest man.

At another time a man named Burnt-tobacco was crossing over the ridge from Nottely to Hemptown in Georgia and heard a drum and the songs of dancers in the hills on one side of the trail. He rode over to see who could be dancing in such a place, but when he reached the spot the drum and the songs were behind him, and he was so frightened that he hurried back to the trail and rode all the way to Hemptown as hard as he could to tell the story. He was a truthful man, and they believed what he said.

There must have been a good many of the Nûñnë'hï living in that neighborhood, because the drumming wits often heard in the high balds almost up to the time of the Removal.

On a small upper branch of Nottely, running nearly due north from Blood maintain, there was also a hole, like a small well or chimney, in the ground, from which there came up a warm vapor that heated all the air around. People said that this was because the Nûñnë'hï had a townhouse and a fire under the mountain. Sometimes in cold weather hunters would stop there to warm the selves, but they were afraid to stay long. This was more than sixty years ago, but the hole is probably there yet.

Close to the old trading path from South Carolina up to the Cherokee Nation, somewhere near the head of Tugaloo, there was formerly a noted circular depression about the size of a townhouse, and waist deep. Inside it was always clean as though swept by unknown hands. Passing traders would throw logs and rocks into it, but would always, on their return, find them thrown far out from the hole. The Indians said it was a Nûñnë'hï townhouse, and never liked to go near the place or even to talk about it, until at last some logs thrown in by the traders were allowed to remain there, and then they concluded that the Nûñnë'hï, annoyed by the persecution of the white men, had abandoned their townhouse forever.

There is another race of spirits, the *Yûñwï Tsunsdi'*, or "Little People," who live in rock eaves on the mountain side. They are little fellows, hardly reaching up to a man's knee, but well shaped and handsome, with long hair falling almost to the ground. They are great wonder workers and are very fond of music, spending half their time drumming and dancing. They are helpful and kind-hearted, and often when people have been lost in the mountains, especially children who have strayed away from their parents, the Yûñwï Tsunsdi' have found them and taken care of -them and brought them back to their homes.

Sometimes their drum is heard in lonely places in the mountains, but it is not safe to follow it, because the Little People do not like to be disturbed at home, and they throw a spell over the stranger so that he is bewildered and loses his way, and even if he does at last get back to the settlement, he is like one dazed ever after.

Sometimes, also, they come near a house at night and the people inside hear them talking, but they must not go out, and in the morning, they find the corn gathered or the field cleared as if a whole force of men had been at work. If anyone should go out to watch, he would die. When a hunter finds anything in the woods, such as a knife or a trinket, he must say, "Little People, I want to take this," because it may belong to them, and if he does not ask their permission, they will throw stones at him as he goes home.

Once a hunter in winter found tracks in the snow like the tracks of little children. He wondered how they could have come there and followed them until they led him to a cave, which was full of Little People, young and old, men, women, and children. They brought him in and were kind to him, and he was with them some time; but when he left, they warned him that he must not tell or he would die.

He went back to the settlement and his friends were all anxious to know where he had been. For a long time, he refused to say, until at last he could not hold out any longer, but told the story, and in a few days he died. Only a few years ago two hunters from Raventown, going behind the high fall near the head of Oconaluftee on the East Cherokee reservation, found there a cave with fresh footprints of the Little People all over the floor.

During the smallpox among the East Cherokee just after the war one sick man wandered off, and his friends searched, but could not find him. After several weeks he came back and said that the Little People had found him and taken him to one of their eaves and tended him until he was cured.

About twenty-five years ago a man named Tsantäwû' was lost in the mountains on the head of Oconaluftee. It was winter time and very cold and his friends thought he must be dead, but after sixteen days he came back and said that the Little People had found him and taken him to their cave, where he had been well treated, and given plenty of everything to eat except bread. This was in large loaves, but when he took them in his hand to eat, they seemed to shrink into small cakes so light and crumbly that though he might eat all day he would not be satisfied.

After he was well rested, they had brought him a part of the way home until they came to a small creek, about knee deep, when they told him to wade across to reach the main trail on the other side. He waded across and turned to look back, but the Little People were gone and the creek was a deep river. When he reached home his legs were frozen to the knees and he lived only a few days.

Once the Yûñwï Tsunsdi' had been very kind to the people of a certain settlement, helping them at night with their work and taking good care of any lost children, until something happened to offend them and they made up their minds to leave the neighborhood. Those who were watching at the time saw the whole company of Little People come down to the ford of the river and cross over and disappear into the mouth of a large cave on the other side. They were never heard of near the settlement again.

There are other fairies, the *Yûñwï Amai'yïnë'hï*, or Water-dwellers, who live in the water, and fishermen pray to them for help. Other friendly spirits live in people's houses, although no one can see them, and so long as they are there to protect the house no witch can come near to do mischief.

Tsäwa'sï and *Tsäga'sï* are the names of two small fairies, who are mischievous enough, but yet often help the hunter who prays to them. Tsäwa'sï, or Tsäwa'sï Usdi'ga (Little Tsäwa'sï), is a tiny fellow, very handsome, with long hair falling down to his feet, who lives in grassy patches on the hillsides and has great power over the game. To the deer hunter who prays to him he gives skill to slip up on the deer through the long grass without being seen. Tsäga'sï is another of the spirits invoked by the hunter and is very helpful, but when someone trips and falls, we know that it is Tsäga'sï who has caused it. There are several other of these fairies with names, all good-natured, but more or less tricky.

Then there is *De'tsätä*. De'tsätä was once a boy who ran away to the woods to avoid a scratching and tries to keep himself invisible ever since. He is a handsome little fellow and spends his whole time hunting birds with blowgun and arrow. He has a great many children who are all just like him and have the same name. When a flock of birds flies up suddenly as if frightened it is because De'tsätä is chasing them. He is mischievous and sometimes hides an arrow from the bird hunter, who may have shot it off into a perfectly clear space, but looks and looks without finding it. Then the hunter says, "De'tsätä, you have my arrow, and if you don't give it up, I'll scratch you," and when he looks again, he finds it.

There is one spirit that goes about at night with a light. The Cherokee call it *Atsil'-dihye'gï*, "The Fire-carrier," and they are all afraid of it, because they think it dangerous, although they do not know much about it. They do not even know exactly what it looks like, because they are afraid to stop when they see it. It may be a witch instead of a spirit. Wafford's mother saw the "Fire-carrier" once when she was a young woman, as she was coming home at night from a trading post in South Carolina. It seemed to be following her from behind, and. she was frightened and whipped up her horse until she got away from it and never saw it again.

The Ghost Woman

Seneca

In a Seneca village there was a young man who was an orphan. He had neither home nor relatives. He lived first with one family and then with another.

One fall, when the men were getting ready to go deer hunting, the young man asked if he could go. The hunters didn't want him and he was left alone.

Then he said, "I'll go by myself," and he started Towards night he came to an opening in the woods and saw a brush house over by the bushes.

He went to the house and looked in; there was no one there. The young man thought that the other hunters had built the house and spent a night there. He went in, kindled a fire, made a place to sleep on, and lay down.

About midnight he heard someone come in and, opening his eyes, he saw a woman. She looked at him but didn't speak, then she moved toward his couch and stopped again.

At last, she said, "I have come to help you. You must not be afraid. I will stay all night in the, cabin."

He said, "If you will help me, you may stay."

"I have passed through this world," said the woman,

I know that you are poor; that you have no relatives and are alone; the hunters didn't want you to go with them. This is why I came to help you. To-morrow start early and travel till it is time to camp, then I will be there."

Towards daylight the woman left the cabin.

In the morning the young man started on. Towards dark, when he thought it was time to stop, he looked for a spring, found one and had just finished his camp when night came.

In the night the woman came as before. The next day the man had good luck. He killed every kind of game.

The woman stayed with him till the hunting season was over. No hunter in the woods had killed as much game as he had. When he was ready to go home the woman said, "I will go with you to the first camp you made."

They spent the night at that camping place. The next morning, she said, "I will stay here. When you get home, everybody will find out that you have brought all kinds of meat and skins. One and another will come to you and say, 'You must marry my daughter,' an old woman will say, 'You must marry my granddaughter.' Don't listen to them. Come back next year and you will have good luck. When you are getting ready, if a man wants to come with you, don't let him. Come alone. We will meet here."

They parted, and the young man continued his journey, carrying on his back a heavy load of game.

In the village he found some of the hunters. Others came soon after. All boasted of the game they had killed.

The young man said, "I will give each man as much meat as he wants, if he will go to my camp and get it."

Many went and brought back all the meat they could carry; still there was meat left.

Every woman who had a daughter or a granddaughter, asked the young man to come and live with them. At last, the chief asked him. to marry his daughter. The man was afraid that if he refused harm would come to him, for the chief was a powerful person. He consented and married the chief's daughter.

When the hunting season came, a great many men, and the chief, who thought his son-in-law was the best hunter in the tribe, wanted to go hunting with him, but he said, "I'm not going, this year."

The hunters started off one after another. When all had gone, the young man went alone to the camp where he was to meet the woman.

Early in the night she came in, stopped by the door, and said, "I am sorry you didn't do as I told you to. I cannot stay with you," and she disappeared.

Day after day the man hunted but he saw no large game. He shot small game, squirrels and birds, for he was hungry. He went back to the village and had to tell the people that he had seen no game.

The woman was a ghost woman.

The Gods and the Six Regions

In ancient times, Po-shai-an-ki-a, the father of the sacred bands, or tribes, lived with his followers in the City of Mists, the Middle Place, guarded by six warriors, the prey gods. Toward the North, he was guarded by Long Tail, the mountain lion; West by Clumsy Foot, the bear; South by Black-Mark Face, the badger; East by Hang Tail, the wolf; above by White Cap, the eagle; below by Mole.

So, when he was about to go forth into the world, he divided the earth into six regions: North, the Direction of the Swept or Barren Plains; West, the Direction of the Home of the Waters; South, the Place of the Beautiful Red; East, the Direction of the Home of Day; upper regions, the Direction of the Home of the High; lower regions, the Direction of the Home of the Low.

How Glooskap made the Elves and Fairies, and then Man of an Ash Tree, and last of all, Beasts, and of his Coming at the Last Day

Passamaquoddy

Glooskap came first of all into this country, into Nova Scotia, Maine, Canada, into the land of the Wabanaki, next to sunrise. There were no Indians here then (only wild Indians very far to the west).

First born were the Mikumwess, the Oonahgemessuk, the small Elves, little men, dwellers in rocks.

And in this way, he made Man: He took his bow and arrows and shot at trees, the basket-trees, the Ash. Then Indians came out of the bark of the Ash-trees.

And then the Mikumwess said . . . called tree-man. . . .

Glooskap made all the animals. He made them at first very large. Then he said to Moose, the great Moose who was as tall as Ketawkqu's, "What would you do should you see an Indian coming?" Moose replied, "I would tear down the

29

trees on him." Then Glooskap saw that the Moose, was too strong, and made him smaller, so that Indians could kill him.

Then he said to the Squirrel, who was of the size of a Wolf. What would you do if you should meet an Indian? And the Squirrel answered, "I would scratch down trees on him." Then Glooskap said, "You also are too strong," and he made him little.

Then he asked the great White Bear what he would do if he met an Indian; and the Bear said, "Eat him." And the Master bade him go and live among rocks and ice, where he would see no Indians.

So, he questioned all the beasts, changing their size or allotting their lives according to their answers.

He took the Loon for his dog; but the Loon absented himself so much that he chose for this service two wolves, --one black and one white. 4 But the Loons are always his tale-bearers.

Many years ago, a man very far to the North wished to cross a bay, a great distance, from one point to another. As he was stepping into his canoe he saw a man with two dogs, --one black and one white, --who asked to be set across. The Indian said, "You may go, but what will become of your dogs?" Then the stranger replied, "Let them go round by land." "Nay," replied the Indian, "that is much too far." But the stranger saying nothing, he put him across. And as they reached the landing place there stood the dogs. But when he turned his head to address the man, he was gone. So, he said to himself, "I have seen Glooskap."

Yet again, --but this was not so many years ago, far in the North there were at a certain place many Indians assembled. And there was a frightful commotion, caused by the ground heaving and rumbling; the rocks shook and fell, they were greatly alarmed, and lo! Glooskap stood before them, and said, "I go away now, but I shall return again; when you feel the ground tremble, then know it is I." So, they will know when the last great war is to be, for then Glooskap will make the ground shake with an awful noise.

Glooskap was no friend of the Beavers; he slew many of them. Up on the Tobaic are two salt-water rocks (that is, rocks by the ocean-side, near a freshwater stream). The Great Beaver, standing there one day, was seen by Glooskap miles away, who had forbidden him that place. Then picking up a large rock where he stood by the shore, he threw it all that distance at the Beaver, who indeed dodged it; but when another came, the beast ran into a mountain, and has never come forth to this day. But the rocks which the master threw are yet to be seen.

This very interesting tradition was taken down by Mrs. W. Wallace Brown from a very old Passamaquoddy Indian woman named Molly Sepsis, who could not speak a word of English, with the aid of another younger woman named Sarah.

It will be observed that it is said in the beginning that Glooskap produced the first human beings from the ash-tree. Ash and Elm in the Edda were the Adam and Eve of the human race. There were no intelligent men on earth--

"Until there came three
mighty and benevolent
Aesir to the world
from their assembly
nearly powerless,

31

Ash and Embla (Ash and Elm),
void of destiny.

"Spirit they possessed not,
sense they had not,
blood nor motive powers,
nor goodly color.
Spirit gave Odin,
sense gave Hoenir,
blood gave Lodur
and good color. "

It is certain, however, that the ash was the typic tree of all life, since the next verse of the Völuspa is devoted to Yggdrasil, the tree of existence, or of the world itself. It may be observed that in the Finnish poem of Kalévala it is by the destruction of the great oak that Wäinämöien, aided by the hero of the sea, causes all things to grow. The early clearing away of trees, as a first step towards culture, may be symbolized in the shooting of arrows at the ash.

The wolf, as a beast for the deity to ride, is strongly Eddaic.

"Magic songs they sung,
rode on Wolves,
the god (Odin) and gods. 1

We have here within a few lines, accordingly, the ash as the parent of mankind, and wolves as the beasts of transport for the supreme deity, both in the Indian legend and in the Edda.

As Glooskap is directly declared in one tradition to keep by him as an attendant a being who is the course of the sun and of the seasons, it may be assumed that the black and white wolf represent day and night.

Again, great stress is laid in the Glooskap legend upon the fact that the last great day of battle with Malsum. the Wolf, and the frost-giants, stone-giants, and other powers of evil, shall be announced by an earthquake.

"Trembles Yggdrasil's
Ash yet standing,
groans that aged tree . . .
and the Wolf runs . . .
The monster's kin goes
all with the Wolf. . . .
Tile stony hills are dashed together,
The giantesses totter.
Then arises Hlin's second grief
When Odin goes
with the wolf to fight."

Word for word, ash-tree, giantesses, the supreme god fighting with a wolf, and falling hills, are given in the Indian myth. This is not the Christian Day of Judgment, but the Norse.

In this myth Glooskap has two wolves, one black and the other white. This is an indication of day and night, since he is distinctly stated to have as an attendant Kulpejotei, who typifies the course of the seasons. In the Eddas (Ragnarok) we are told that one wolf now follows the, sun, another the moon; one Fenris, the other Moongarm:—

"The moon's devourer
In a troll's disguise."

The magic arrows of Glooskap are of course worldwide, and date from the shafts of Abaris and those used among the ancient Jews for divination. But it may be observed that those of the Indian hero are like the "Guse arrows," described in Oervarodd's Saga, which always hit their mark and return to the one who shoots them.

It is important here to compare this *old* Algonquin account of the Creation with that of the Iroquois, or Six Nations, as given by David Cusick, himself an Indian: —

"There was a woman who was with child, with twins. She descended from the higher world, and was received on the turtle. While she was in the distress of travail, one of the infants in her womb was moved by an evil desire, and determined to pass out under the side of the parent's arm, and the other infant endeavored in vain to prevent his design. They entered the dark world by compulsion, and their mother expired in a few minutes. One of them possessed a gentle disposition, and was named Enigorio, the Good Mind. The other possessed an insolence of character, and was called Enigonhahetgea; that is, the Bad Mind. The Good Mind was not content to remain in a dark situation, and was desirous to create a great light in the dark world; but the Bad Mind was desirous that the world should remain in its original state. The Good Mind, determined to prosecute his design, began the work of creation. Of his mother's head he made the sun, of her body the moon.

After he had made creeks and rivers, animals and fishes, he formed two images of the dust of the ground in his own likeness, male and female, and by his breathing into their nostrils he gave them living souls, and named them *ea gwe howe*, that is a real people; and he gave the Great Island all the animals--of game for the inheritance of the people. . .. The Bad Mind, while his brother was making the universe, went through the island, and made numerous high mountains and falls of water and great steeps, and also created reptiles which would be injurious to mankind; but the Good Mind restored the island to its former condition. The Bad Mind made two images of clay in the form of mankind, but while he was giving them existence, they became *apes*. The Good Mind discovered his brother's contrivances, and aided in giving them living souls.

"Finding that his brother continually thwarted him, the Good Mind admonished him to behave better. The Bad Mind then offered a challenge to his brother, on condition that the victor should rule the universe. The Good Mind was willing. He falsely mentioned that whipping with flags [bulrushes] would destroy his *temporal* life, and earnestly solicited his brother to observe the instrument of death, saying that by using deer-horns he would expire. [This is very obscure in Cusick's Indian-English.] On the day appointed the battle began; it lasted for two days; they tore up the trees and mountains; at last, the Good Mind gained the victory by using the horns. The last words uttered by the Bad Mind were that he would have equal power over the souls of mankind after their death, and so sank down to eternal doom and became the Evil Spirit."

Contrasted with this hardly heathen cosmogony, which shows recent Bible influence throughout, the Algonquin narrative reads like a song from the Edda. That the latter is the original and the older there can be no doubt. Between the "Good Mind," making man "from the dust of the earth," and Glooskap, rousing him by magic arrows from the ash-tree, there is a great difference. It may be observed that the fight with horns is explained in another legend in this book, called the Chenoo, and that these horns are the magic horns of the Chepitch calm, or Great Serpent, who is somewhat like the dragon.

In the Algonquin story, two Loons are Glooskap's "tale-bearers," which occasion him great anxiety by their prolonged absences. This is distinctly stated in the Indian legend, as it is of Odin's birds in the Edda. Odin has, as news-bringers, two ravens.

"Hugin and Munin
Fly each day
over the spacious earth.
I fear for Hugin
that he comes not back,
yet more anxious am I
for Munin."

The Loons, indeed, occasioned Glooskap so much trouble by absences that he took wolves in their place. The ravens of the Edda are probably of biblical origin. But it is a most extraordinary coincidence that the Indians have a corresponding perversion of Scripture, for they say that Glooskap, when he was in the ark, that is as Noah, sent out a white dove, which returned to him colored black, and became a raven. This is not, however, related as part of the myth.

The Ancient History of the Six Nations, by David Cusick, gives us in one particular a strange coincidence with the Edda. It tells us that the Bad Mind, the principle of Evil, forced himself out into life, as Cusick expresses it in his broken Indian-English, "under the side of the parent's arm;" that is, through the armpit. In the Edda (Vafthrudnismal, 33) we are told of the first beings born on earth that they were twins, begotten by the two feet of a giant, and born out of his armpit.

"Under the armpit grew,
't is said of the Hrîmthurs,
a girl and boy together;
foot with foot begat,
of that wise Jötun,
a six-headed son."

There are in these six lines six coincidences with red Indian mythology: The Evil principle as a Jötun's first-born in the one and the Bad Mind in the other are born of the mother's armpit. In one of the tales of Lox, the Indian devil, also a giant, we are told that his feet are male and female. In both faiths this is the first birth on earth. The six-headed demon appears in a Micmac tale. There is in both the Eddaic and the Wabanaki account a very remarkable coincidence in this: that there is a Titanic or giant birth of twins on earth, followed by the creation of man from the ash-tree. The Evil principle, whether it be the Wolf-Lox in the Wabanaki myths, or Loki in the Norse, often turns himself into a woman. Thus, the male and female sex of the first-born twins is identified.

According to the Edda, the order of births on earth was as follows: —

First, two giants were born from the mother's armpit.

Secondly, the dwarfs were created.

Thirdly, man was made from the ash-tree.

According to the Wabanaki, this was the order: —

First, two giants were born, *one* from his mother's armpit.

Secondly, the dwarfs (Mikumwessuk) were created from the bark of the ash-tree.

Thirdly, man was made from the *trunk* of the ash.

The account of the creation of the dwarfs is wanting in the present manuscript.

Wíshakon and His Friend Visit the Plèthoak (Thunderers)

Delaware

An old man and a little boy lived together with great affection. They were not relatives; they called each other "Friend."

One day the old man put on new moccasins, fixed new feathers in his head-dress, trimmed his hair and painted his face.

The little boy, watching him, asked, "What are you going to do, my friend?"

"I'm going on a long journey; I want to see what there is in the world."

"May I go with you?"

"If your father and mother are willing."

The boy asked his parents and they gave their consent. His friend gave him a new bow and arrows, trimmed his hair,

painted his face and put a new feather in his headdress.
Then they set out together.

When night came, they made a fire in the woods, ate and
slept.

They traveled many days. At last, they came to a lake so
broad that they could not cross it.

"How can we get to the other side?" asked the boy.

"We'll make a canoe," said his friend.

Will it take long to make a canoe?"

"It will not."

The old man looked around in the woods till he found a
hickory tree. He pulled the tree up, stripped the bark off
and made a large canoe. The next morning, they put their
bows and arrows into the canoe and started to cross the
lake. Toward night they came to a low island and, without
going on shore, they fastened their canoe to the bullrushes.

"How can we sleep here?" asked the boy. "Maybe in the
water there are creatures that will come out and kill us."

"We are safe here," said the old man.

"If the wind blows, we will be carried out into the lake,"
said the boy.

"The wind will not blow.

The boy and his friend lay down and fell asleep. About
midnight the boy heard the water roar and it seemed to him

that the canoe was moving swiftly. He thought the wind was blowing. He sat up. It was clear overhead, and the wind wasn't blowing.

"The water must be running very fast," thought the boy; and putting his hand out he touched the water and found that it was going with great swiftness. He roused the old man by reaching his feet and shaking them.

"Get up, friend," said he, "something is the trouble. The water is running by very fast. Where is the lake going?"

"Lie down," said the old man, "no harm will come to us."

The boy lay down, but couldn't sleep. Just at daybreak a voice spoke to him, and, opening his eyes, he saw a fine-looking man, ornamented with paint and feathers. He saw also that the canoe was on dry land.

The stranger wakened the old man, and said, "Come with me!"

Taking their bows and arrows the old man and the boy followed the stranger, who led them to a long house. 1 There were many persons inside, some asleep, some awake. When the old man of the house met them, he said to their guide, "Oh, you have brought them?"

Then he turned to the two friends, and said, "I am glad that you have come. You have heard of us. We are the people whom you call Thunder. We bring rain to make corn and beans and squashes grow. We put it in your mind to come on this journey from the East. We want you to help us. You are more powerful than we are. We want you to kill some of our enemies."

Old man Thunder placed food before the friends, corn beans, and squash, and said, "We have plenty of this food. We take a little from a great many fields. When you see a small or withered squash, or bad kernels of corn on an ear, or dried-up beans in a pod you may know that we have taken our part from them. We have taken the spirit and left the shell. If you see a whole field of withered corn, you may know that we have taken the spirit from it, but we seldom destroy a whole field; we take only a little."

After the friends had eaten, the old chief said, "On a hill is a great hemlock tree. On that tree is a porcupine of enormous size. He hurls his quills and kills everyone who approaches him. We Thunders are afraid to go near the tree. We want you to destroy this porcupine."

As they started for the hill the little boy went ahead. The old man and the Thunders laughed to see him, and the old man said, "I think my little friend might try his luck first." The boy heard this and was greatly pleased.

They stopped some distance from the tree. No one would venture near it. The boy went into the ground and forward till he was directly under the porcupine. Then he put his head and arms out of the ground, took aim and sent an arrow into the porcupine's body. The porcupine moved a little. The boy sent another arrow, and still another. The porcupine, feeling something, raised up his quills and shot them off in every direction, then groaned, rolled from the tree, and fell to the ground dead.

The Thunders came up, cut open the porcupine, took out its entrails, and ate its flesh.

All wondered at the power of the little boy. Old man Thunder said, "We have another enemy, a sunfish that lives in our river here and lets no one come near for water.

The boy said, "I can kill him."

The next day the Thunders and the old man went near enough to show the boy where the sunfish lived. A great tree had fallen into the river, under the trunk of this tree the sunfish had its home. The boy saw the fish. He sent an arrow and the arrow went straight to the heart of the sunfish and the sunfish came to the surface and died. The Thunders sprang into the water, pulled the body out and dragged it off to Old Thunder's house.

The next day, Old Thunder said, "We have one more enemy. Every day there flies past here a creature as big as a cloud. He brings sickness here and many of our people die. If we could kill this creature, few of us would die. He passes here from the West, early in the morning, and goes back in the evening."

The next morning the old man and the boy went out and hid in the grass. Soon they saw the creature coming from the West. When it was over the place where the two were hidden, the boy sent an arrow into its body. The creature didn't fall, but it turned and went slowly back in the direction from which it came.

Old man Thunder was very thankful. He said to the two friends, "You may stay here and live with us."

The old man said, "I cannot help you, but my little friend, WÍSHAKON, may stay. He is so powerful that he will be of great assistance to you."

"We will go to your place to-night," said old man Thunder. "We will carry you with us in the clouds."

When they came to the old man's place, the council house was full of people. As Thunders entered, they began to dance. When they shook their heads. lightning flashed around the room.

The chiefs said, "Our grandfathers are here to-night. They may do us harm."

For a little while Thunders quieted down. Again, they got excited in the dance and shook their heads till lightning flashed everywhere and the people were frightened. When they had danced as long as they wanted to, they went home, leaving the old man, but taking WÍSHAKON with them, and to this day the little boy goes with them everywhere.

After the great Thunders roar, we hear the little fellow with his alto voice, and we say, "That is WÍSHAKON, and we burn tobacco saying, "This is all we have to give," and we thank him for rain.

The Raven Mocker

Cherokee

Of all the Cherokee wizards or witches, the most dreaded is the Raven Mocker (*Kâ'lanû Ahkyeli'skï*), the one that robs the dying man of life. They are of either sex and there is no sure way to know one, though they usually look withered and old, because they have added so many lives to their own.

At night, when some one is sick or dying in the settlement, the Raven Mocker goes to the place to take the life. He flies through the air in fiery shape, with arms outstretched like wings, and sparks trailing behind, and a rushing sound like the noise of a strong wind. Every little while as he flies, he makes a cry like the cry of a raven when it "dives" in the air--not like the common raven cry--and those who hear are afraid, because they know that some man's life will soon go out. When the Raven Mocker comes to the house, he finds others of his kind waiting there, and unless there is a doctor on guard who knows how to drive them away, they go inside, all invisible, and frighten and torment the sick man until they kill him. Sometimes to do this they even lift him from the bed and throw him on the floor, but his friends who are with him think he is only struggling for breath.

After the witches kill him, they take out his heart and eat it, and so add to their own lives as many days or years as they have taken from his. No one in the room can see them, and there is no sear where they take out the heart, but yet there is no heart left in the body. Only one who has the right medicine can recognize a Raven Mocker, and if such a man stays in the room with the sick person these witches are afraid to come in, and retreat as soon as they see him, because when one of them is recognized in his right shape he must die within seven days. There was once a man named Gûñskäli'skï, who had this medicine and used to hunt for Raven Mockers, and killed several. When the friends of a dying person know that there is no more hope, they always try to have one of these medicine men stay in the house and watch the body until it is buried, because after burial the witches do not steal the heart.

The other witches are jealous of the Raven Mockers and afraid to come into the same house with one. Once a man who had the witch medicine was watching by a sick man and saw these other witches outside trying to get in. All at once they heard a Raven Mocker cry overhead and the others scattered "like a flock of pigeons when the hawk swoops." When at last a Raven Mocker dies these other witches sometimes take revenge by digging up the body and abusing it.

The following is told on the reservation as an actual happening:

A young man had been out on a hunting trip and was on his way home when night came on while he was still a long distance from the settlement. He knew of a house not far off the trail where an old man and his wife lived, so he turned in that direction to look for a place to sleep until morning. When he got to the house there was nobody in it. He looked into the âsï and found no one there either. He thought maybe they had gone after water, and so stretched himself out in the farther corner to sleep. Very soon he heard a raven cry outside, and in a little while afterwards the old man came into the âsï and sat down by the fire without noticing the young man, who kept still in the dark corner. Soon there was another raven cry outside, and the old man said to himself, "Now my wife is coming," and sure enough in a little while the old woman came in and sat down by her husband. Then the young man knew they were Raven Mockers and he was frightened and kept very quiet.

Said the old man to his wife, "Well, what luck did you have?" "None," said the old woman, "there were too many doctors watching. What luck did you have?" "I got what I went for," said the old man, "there is no reason to fail, but you never have luck. Take this and cook it and lees have something to eat." She fixed the fire and then the young man smelled meat roasting and thought it smelled sweeter than any meat he had ever tasted. He peeped out from one eye, and it looked like a man's heart roasting on a stick.

Suddenly the old woman said to her husband, "Who is over in the corner?" "Nobody," said the old man. "Yes, there is," said the old woman, "I hear him snoring," and she stirred the fire until it blazed and lighted up the whole place, and there was the young man lying in the corner. He kept quiet and pretended to be asleep. The old man made a noise at the fire to wake him, but still he pretended to sleep. Then the old man came over and shook him, and he sat up and rubbed his eyes as if he had been asleep all the time.

Now it was near daylight and the old woman was out in the other house getting breakfast ready, but the hunter could hear her crying to herself. "Why is your wife crying?" he asked the old man. "Oh, she has lost some of her friends lately and feels lonesome," said her husband; but the young man knew that she was crying because he had heard them talking.

When they came out to breakfast the old man put a bowl of corn mush before him and said, "This is all we have--we have had no meat for a long time." After breakfast the young man started on again, but when he had gone a little way, the old man ran after him with a fine piece of beadwork and gave it to him, saying, "Take this, and don't tell anybody what you heard last, night, because my wife and I are always quarreling that way." The young man took the piece, but when he came to the first creek, he threw it into the water and then went on to the settlement. There he told the whole story, and a party of warriors started back with him to kill the Raven Mockers. When they reached the place, it was seven days after the first night. They found the old man and his wife lying dead in the house, so they set fire to it and burned it and the witches together.

The Giants from the West

Cherokee

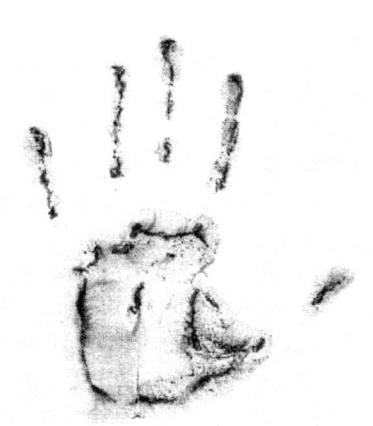

James Wafford, of the western Cherokee, who was born in Georgia in 1806, says that his grandmother, who must have been born about the middle of the last century, told him that she had beard from the old people that long before her time a party of giants had come once to visit the Cherokee. They were nearly twice as tall as common men, and had their eyes set slanting in their heads, so that the Cherokee called them Tsunil'kälû', "The Slant-eyed people," because they looked like the giant hunter Tsul'kälû' (see the story). They said that these giants lived very far away in the direction in which the sun goes down. The Cherokee received them as friends, and they stayed some time, and then returned to their home in the west. The story may be a distorted historical tradition.

The Young Woman and Thunder

Seneca - Told by George Titus

One day a stranger went into a cabin where a man and his wife and four children lived and asked to marry the youngest daughter of the family. The father and mother consented and the stranger married the girl.

After a time, he asked his wife to go home with him; her parents were willing and the two started. They hadn't gone far when they came to a cabin and the young man said, "This is my home."

There was nobody in the cabin when the husband and wife came but toward night the woman heard some one coming on the run. Soon a man came in and sat down by the door. Again, she heard running; another man came in and sat down; then a third man came.

The three men began talking with one another, relating how far they had traveled and what they had killed.

One said, "I had good luck, I killed a bear."

Finding that he was the only one who had killed anything, the two said, "Go and bring the bear. We'll cook it."

The young woman sat at the opposite end of the room, watching. She saw the man bring in what he called a bear, saw that it was the trunk and head of a man's body. The men cut it up and put it in a kettle to boil. When cooked they ate it.

The three walked back and forth in the room without looking toward the woman. Her husband was there but he didn't talk or eat with the men. They were his brothers but he never ate their kind of food.

Each morning the three brothers went to hunt for game. in the evening they came back and sitting down near the door talked over their journey. Then, if they had killed any game, they brought it into the cabin, cooked and ate it. If they had no game, they ate what was left from the meal of the previous evening.

One day when the young woman went for water, she found a man standing by the spring. The man said to her, "I have come to tell you that to-morrow your husband is going into the ground. As soon as he goes put some of your spittle exactly in the center of the cabin and tell it to answer for you every time your husband speaks. When you have done that hurry to this place."

The next morning the young man said to his wife, "I am going into the ground and I want you to stay in the cabin all the time I am away." He turned around and right where he stood, he disappeared.

After doing as she had been told, the woman went to the spring; the stranger was there. Taking an arrow he put the woman into the head of it, and saying, "When the arrow falls, jump out and hurry along the lake, as fast as you can." He shot the arrow into the air.

The husband called to his wife, "Are you there?"

"I am here" answered the spittle.

After a time he called again, "Are you there?"

"I am here," was the answer.

The man was away a number of days and he often asked, "Are you there?" and always received the same answer. When he came above ground and asked, "Where are you, wife?" and her voice answered, "I am here," he looked around but didn't see her, then he found what had been talking to him.

He was terribly angry and right away began to hunt for the woman's tracks. He found them and followed them to the spring, but there they disappeared. He hunted a long time, then, getting discouraged, he called his dog O^{n}HDAGWÍJA (Good Ear), and said, "You didn't take care of my wife while I was gone. Now you must find her."

The man watched the dog. It ran around and around and came back to the spring, then it stopped hunting on the ground, looked up in the air, sniffed and ran toward the North, looking up all the time as if it saw tracks. The man followed the dog. After a while the two came to where the arrow fell, then there were tracks on the ground.

The dog barked and began to run faster, the man urging it on. When they were about to overtake the woman, the stranger who had been at the spring stood in front of her.

Putting her into an arrow, he said, "You will come down on an island in a lake. Run across the island in every direction. I will be there."

When the man and dog came to where the woman met the stranger, they lost her tracks. Again, the dog ran around smelling the ground, then looking up in the air he saw a trail and followed it.

When Good Ear and his master came to the lake the man changed to a flea and went into the hair behind the dog's ear.

The dog swam to the island, the flea became a man and the two traveled on till they came to where the arrow fell. There they found the woman's tracks and followed their across and around the island.

When they were overtaking the woman the stranger stood in front of her, and, putting her into an arrow, said, "You will come down on the shore of the lake. Run as fast as you can. I can do nothing more for you, but you will soon come to a village and there you will find some one to help you. Now you may know who I am."

As the stranger turned to go the woman saw that he was DJONKDJO^{n}KWE^n (Chickadee).

When the dog came to where the tracks disappeared on the ground, he saw the trail in the air and knew that the woman had crossed the lake. Again, the man turned to flea and hid in the dog's hair. The dog swam to the shore; the flea became a man, and the two followed the woman's footprints.

When her husband was so near that the woman could hear the dog bark, she came to a house. A man was sitting inside making arrow-heads. The man was OTHÄGWE^{n}DONIS (Flintmaker). When the woman asked him to help her, he said, "I will do what I can, but hurry along, the man in the next house will help you."

When the dog came Flintmaker threw a handful of arrow-heads at him. Wherever the arrow-heads struck they tore up the trees and the ground, but the dog dodged them all, ran at Flintmaker, caught him by the throat and shook him till he was dead.

At the second house the woman found a man making nets. This man was HADÄE′ONIS (Netmaker).

The woman said to him, "I am running away from a bad man. I want you to help me."

"I'll do what I can," said HADÄE′ONIS, "but hurry on. You will soon come to a house, the people who live there will help you."

When the dog and the man came, HADÄE′ONIS threw out a net. It caught the two and wound around and around them. For a long time, they struggled to free themselves. At last, the dog broke through the net, ran at HADÄE′ONIS, caught him by the throat and shook him till he was dead.

In the third house the woman found four brothers. When she asked them for help, they went out and chopping down dry trees piled them on her tracks. When they had a high pile, they set it afire, and standing, two at each side of the pile, they waited.

The dog and the man came to the fire, the dog wanted to go around but the man saw that the tracks led into the fire and he said, "No! You must go through."

The dog sprang into the fire and the man followed. When they came out on the other side both dog and man were almost dead. The eldest of the four brothers said, "We will shoot them."

They shot, but arrows had no effect. all Then the old man said, "We must catch them, kill them, and pull their hearts out."

They caught the man and the dog, killed them, pulled out their hearts and put the hearts in a red-hot kettle that the old man had heated over the fire. The hearts flew around and around trying to get out of the kettle but the brothers pushed them down and shot at them till they were dead and burned to ashes.

The old man, whose name was DÉONĒYONT (Red-hot) went to the house and told the woman she was safe. He said to her, "You must rest four days then go home."

When the fourth day came, Red-hot said, "It is time to go. Your home is in the South. As you travel you will know where you are."

The woman started. About midday she met a stranger who said, "Towards night you will find something to eat."

She traveled till the sun went down, then came to a large stump and found there a pot of hulled corn cooked with bear meat, she thought, "This must be what the man meant." She ate the hulled corn and meat then went on till dark. That night she camped under a tree.

The next morning the woman started again. At midday she met the stranger and he told her that she would soon find something to eat. Towards night she came to a stump and found there a pot of hulled corn and bear meat.

The next morning when the woman woke up, the stranger was standing by her. He said, "You are near your father's home and I shall leave you now. I am the one whom men call HÍ′NO' (Thunder)."

The stranger disappeared and the woman went on till she came in sight of an old house. Then she saw a spring and right away she knew it was the spring where she used to get water. In the house she found her father and mother. They were glad to see her and said "*Yâwe*ⁿ."

How Glooskap, leaving the World, all the Animals Mourned for him, and how, ere he Departed, he gave Gifts to Men

Micmac

Now Glooskap had freed the world from all the mighty monsters of an early time: the giants wandered no longer in the wilderness; the *cullo* terrified man no more, as it spread its wings like the cloud between him and the sun; the dreadful Chenoo of the North devoured him not; no evil beasts, devils, and serpents were to be found near his home. And the Master had, moreover, taught men the arts which made them happier; but they were not grateful to him, and though they worshiped him they were not the less wicked.

"Now when the ways of men and beasts waxed evil, they greatly vexed Glooskap, and at length he could no longer endure them, and he made a rich feast by the shore of the great Lake Minas. All the beasts came to it, and when the feast was over, he got into a great canoe, and the beasts

looked after him till they saw him no more. And after they
ceased to see him, they still heard his voice as he sang; but
the sounds grew fainter and fainter in the distance, and at
last they wholly died away; and then deep silence fell on
them all, and a great marvel came to pass, and the beasts,
who had till now spoken but one language, were no longer
able to understand each other, and they fled away, each his
own way, and never again have they met together in
council. Until the day when Glooskap shall return to restore
the Golden Age, and make men and animals dwell once
more together in amity and peace, all Nature mourns. And
tradition says that on his departure from Acadia the Great
Snowy Owl retired to the deep forests, to return no more
until he could come to welcome Glooskap; and in those
sylvan depths the owls even yet repeat to the night *Koo-
koo-skoos*! which is to say in the Indian tongue, 'Oh, I am
sorry! Oh, I am sorry!' And the Loons, who had been the
huntsmen of Glooskap, go restlessly up and down through
the world, seeking vainly for their master, whom they
cannot find, and wailing sadly because they find him not."

But ere the Master went away from life, or ceased to
wander in the ways of men, he bade it be made known by
the Loons, his faithful messengers, that before his departure
years would pass, and that whoever would seek him might
have one wish granted, whatever that wish might be. Now,
though the journey was long and the trials were terrible
which those must endure who would find Glooskap, there
were still many men who adventured them.

Now ye shall hear who some of these were and what
happened to them. And this is the first tale as it was told me
in the tent of John Gabriel, the Passamaquoddy.

When all men had heard that Glooskap would grant a wish
to any one who would come to him, three Indians resolved

to try this thing; and one was a Maliseet from St. John, and the other two were Penobscots from Old Town. And the path was long and the way was hard, and they suffered much, and they were seven years on it ere they came to him. But while they were yet three months' journey from his dwelling, they heard the barking of his dogs, and as they drew nearer, day by day, it was louder. And so, after great trials, they found the lord of men and beasts, and he made them welcome and entertained them.

But, ere they went, he asked them what they wanted. And the eldest, who was an honest, simple man, and of but little account among his people, because he was a bad hunter, asked that he might excel in the killing and catching of game. Then the Master gave him a flute, or the magic pipe, which pleases every ear, and has the power of persuading every animal to follow him who plays it. And he thanked the lord, and left.

Now the second Indian, being asked what he would have, replied, The love of many women. And when Glooskap, asked how many, he said, "I care not how many, so that there are but enough of them, and more than enough." At hearing this the Master seemed displeased, but, smiling anon, he gave him a bag which was tightly tied, and told him not to open it until he had reached his home. So, he thanked the lord, and left.

Now the third Indian was a gay and handsome but foolish young fellow, whose whole heart was set on making people laugh, and on winning a welcome at every merry-making. And he, being asked what he would have or what he chiefly wanted, said that it would please him most to be able to make a certain quaint and marvelous sound or noise, which was frequent in those primitive times among all the Wabanaki, and which it is said may even yet be heard in a few sequestered wigwams far in the wilderness, away from men; there being still here and there a deep magician, or man of mystery, who knows the art of producing it. And the property of this wondrous sound is such that they who hear it must need burst into a laugh; whence it is the cause that the men of these our modern times are so sorrowful, since that sound is no more heard in the land. And to him Glooskap, was also affable, sending Marten into the woods to seek a certain mystical and magic root, which when eaten would make the miracle the young man sought. But he warned him not to touch the root ere he got to his home, or it would be the worse for him. And so, he thanked the lord, and left.

It had taken seven years to come, but seven days were all that was required to tread the path returning to their home, that is, for him who got there. Only one of all the three beheld his lodge again. This was the hunter, who, with his pipe in his pocket, and not a care in his heart, trudged through the woods, satisfied that so long as he should live, there would always be venison in the larder.

But he who loved women, and had never won even a wife, was filled with anxious wishfulness. And he had not gone very far into the woods before he opened the bag. And there flew out by hundreds, like white doves, swarming all about him, beautiful girls, with black burning eyes and flowing hair. And wild with passion the winsome witches threw their arms about him, and kissed him as he responded to their embraces; but they came ever more and more, wilder and more passionate. And he bade them give way, but they would not, and he sought to escape, but he could not; and so, panting, crying for breath, smothered, he perished. And those who came that way found him dead, but what became of the girls no man knows.

Now the third went merrily onward alone, when all at once it flashed upon his mind that Glooskap had given him a present, and without the least heed to the injunction that he was to wait till he had reached his home drew out the root and ate it; and scarce had he done this ere he realized that he possessed the power of uttering the weird and mystic sound to absolute perfection. And as it rang o'er many a hill and dale, and woke the echoes of the distant hills, until 't was answered by the solemn owl, he felt that it was indeed wonderful. So, he walked on gayly, trumpeting as he went, over hill and vale, happy as a bird.

But by and by he began to weary of himself. Seeing a deer, he drew an arrow and stealing silently to the game was just about to shoot, when despite himself the wild, unearthly sound broke forth like a demon's warble. The deer bounded away, and the young man cursed! And when he reached Old Town, half dead with hunger, he was worth little to make laughter, though the honest, Indians at first did not fail to do so, and thereby somewhat cheered his heart. But as the days went on, they wearied of him, and, life becoming a burden, he went into the woods and slew himself. And the evil spirit of the night-air, even Bumole, 1 or Pamola, from whom came the gift, swooped down from the clouds and bore him away to 'Lahmkekqu', the dwelling place of darkness, and he was no more heard of among men.

As regards the destruction of the giants by Glooskap, it may be observed that the same tradition exists among the Six Nations. Cusick tells us that about 1250 years before Columbus discovered America a powerful tribe called Otne-yar-heh, that is, Stone Giants, who were ravenous cannibals, overran the country, and nearly exterminated the inhabitants. These Stone Giants practiced themselves in rolling on the sand; by this means their bodies became hard. Then Tas-enyawa-gon, the Holder of the Heavens, came to earth as a giant, and, being made their chief, led them into a hollow, where he overwhelmed them with rocks. Only one escaped to the far North.

The reader will recognize in these the Chenoos, or Kewahqu', who cover themselves with pitch and roll on the ground. But no one can deny that, while that which Cusick narrates has much in common with the mythology of the Wabanaki, it is much less like that of the Edda; that Indian grotesqueness has in it greatly perverted an original; and finally, that it certainly occupies a position midway between the mythology of the Northeastern Algonquins and that of the Chippewas, Ottawas, and other Western tribes. Examination shows this in every story. Thus, the Wabanaki warrior makes his bow infallible in aim by stringing it with a cord made of his sister's hair. This is Norse, as it was of old Latin. But in the Iroquois the young man "adorns his arms with the hairs of his sister." Here the tradition has begun to weaken.

It may be interesting to visitors to Niagara to know that the army of Stone Giants crossed the river during their journey just below the Falls.

Tsuwe'nähï: A Legend of Pilot Knob

Cherokee

In the old town of Känuga, on Pigeon River, there was a lazy fellow named Tsuwe'nähï, who lived from house to house among his relatives and never brought home any game, although he used to spend nearly all his time in the woods. At last, his friends got very tired of keeping him, so he told them to get some parched corn ready for him and he would go and bring back a deer or else would never trouble them again. They filled his pouch with parched corn, enough for a long trip, and he started off for the mountains. Day after day passed until they thought they had really seen the last of him, but before the month was half gone, he was back again at Känuga, with no deer, but with a wonderful story to tell.

He said that he had hardly turned away from the trail to go up the ridge when he met a stranger, who asked him where he was going. Tsuwe'nähï answered that his friends in the settlement had driven him out because he was no good hunter, and that if he did not find a deer this time he would never go back again. "Why not come with me?" said the stranger, "my town is not far from here, and you have relatives there." Tsuwe'nähï was very glad of the chance, because he was ashamed to go back to his own town; so, he went with the stranger, who took him to Tsuwa`tel'da (Pilot knob). They came to a cave, and the other said, "Let us go in here;" but the cave ran clear to the heart of the mountain, and when they were inside the hunter found there an open country like a wide bottom land, with a great settlement and hundreds of people. They were all glad to see him. and brought him to their chief, who took him into his own house and showed him a seat near the fire. Tsuwe'nähï sat down, but he felt it move under him, and when he looked again, he saw that it was a turtle, with its head sticking out from the shell. He jumped up, but the chief said, "It won't hurt you; it only wants to see who you are." So, he sat down very carefully, and the turtle drew in its head again. They brought food of the same kind that he had been accustomed to at home, and when he had eaten the chief took him through the settlement until he had seen all the houses and talked with most of the people. When he had seen everything and had rested some days, he was anxious to get back to his home, so the chief himself brought him to the mouth of the cave and showed him the trail that led down to the river. Then he said, "You are going back to the settlement, but you will never be satisfied there any more. Whenever you want to come to us, you know the way." The chief left him, Tsuwe'nähï went down the mountain and along the river until he came to Känuga.

He told his story, but no one believed it and the people only laughed at him. After that, he would go away very often and be gone for several days at a time, and when he came back to the settlement, he would say he had been with the mountain people. At last, one man said he believed the story and would go with him to see. They went off together to the woods, where they made a camp, and then

Tsuwe'nähï went on ahead, saying he would be back soon. The other waited for him, doing a little hunting near the camp, and two nights afterwards Tsuwe'nähï was back again. He seemed to be alone, but was talking as he came, and the other hunter heard girls' voices, although he could see no one. When he came up to the fire he said, "I have two friends with me, and they say there is to be a dance in their town in two nights, and if you want to go, they will come for you." The hunter agreed at once, and Tsuwe'nähï called out, as if to some one close by, "He says he will go." Then he said, "Our sisters have come for some venison." The hunter had killed a deer and had the meat drying over the fire, so he said, "What kind do they want?" The voices answered, "Our mother told us to ask for some of the ribs," but still he could see nothing. He took down some rib pieces and -gave them to Tsuwe'nähï, who took them and said, "In two days we shall come again for you." Then he started off, and the other heard the voices going through the woods until all was still again.

In two days Tsuwe'nähï came, and this time he had two girls with him. As they stood near the fire the hunter noticed that their feet were short and round, almost like dogs' paws, but as soon as they saw him looking, they sat down so that he could not see their feet. After supper the whole party left the camp and went up along the creek to Tsuwa`tel'da. They went in through the cave door until they got to the farther end and could see houses beyond, when all at once the hunter's legs felt as if they were dead and he staggered and fell to the ground. The others lifted him up, but still he could not stand, until the medicine-man brought some "old tobacco" and rubbed it on his legs and made him smell it until he sneezed. Then he was able to stand again and went in with the others. He could not stand at first, because he had not prepared himself by fasting before he started.

The dance had not yet begun and Tsuwe'nähï took the hunter into the townhouse and showed him a seat near the fire, but it had long thorns of honey locust sticking out from it and he was afraid to sit down. Tsuwe'nähï told him not to be afraid, so he sat down and found that the thorns were as soft as down feathers. Now the drummer came. in and the dancers, and the dance began. One man followed at the end of the line, crying *Kû! Kû!* all the time, but not dancing. The hunter wondered, and they told him, "This man was lost in the mountains and had been calling all through the woods for his friends until his voice failed and he was only able to pant *Kû! Kû!* and then we found him and took him in."

When it was over Tsuwe'nähï and the hunter went back to the settlement. At the next dance in Känuga they told all they had seen at Tsuwa`tel'da, what a large town was there and how kind everybody was, and this time--because there were two of them--the people believed it. Now others wanted to go, but Tsuwe'nähï told them they must first fast seven days, while he went ahead to prepare everything, and then he would come and bring them. He went away and the others fasted, until at the end of seven days he came for them and they went with him to Tsuwa`tel'da, and their friends in the settlement never saw them again.

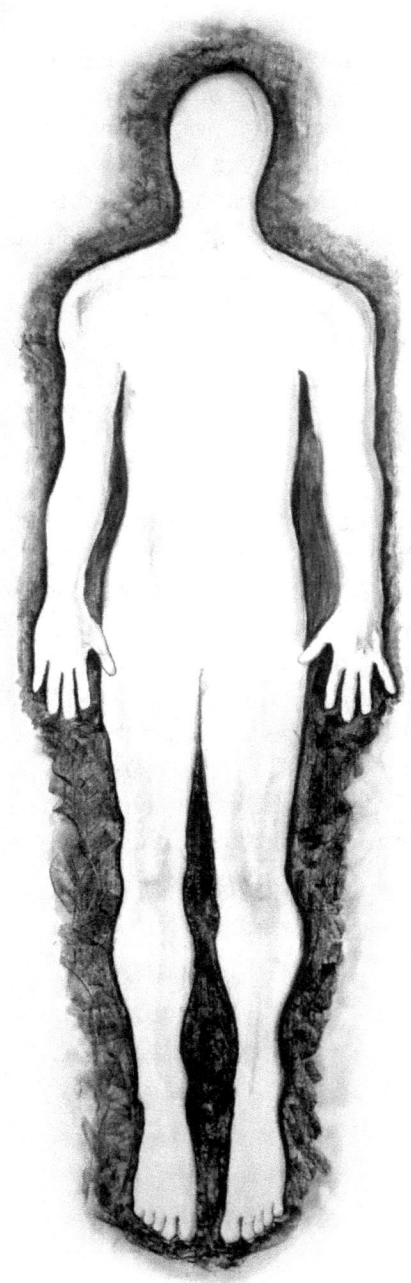

When the Storm God Rides

Tejas

The shores of Texas along the Gulf of Mexico did not always have islands along them. The Indians who lived a long time ago on the coast have left behind them the story of a god and his great black-winged thunder bird which he rode like a horse over the Gulf at certain times. He was the Storm God, and he made islands where none had been before. These islands were made as homes for the wild birds, the sea gulls, the big pelicans, the cranes and the herons.

The god of storms did not live among the Indians, but lived down in the warm seas below the Gulf of Mexico. And for this the Indians were glad, for his terrible thunder bird, named Hurakan, filled the people with fear. The tribes which lived near the Gulf only saw the mighty god when he rode his thunder bird through the skies. He visited their land when he wanted to get the white and colored feathers of birds living on the seashore for his cloak. The Indians could tell when he was on the way. As Hurakan, the thunder bird, came swiftly through the air over the gulf, the sky in front of him became filled with bits of white clouds sailing high over the beaches. Then the wind began to blow, first here, then there. At last came the great thunder bird in the shape of a cloud which closed the eye of the sun and made the land dark. Then the wind grew strong and howled and blew as the god and his thunder bird came flying through the sky. The Indians ran into their wigwams and held them down as best they could while the Storm God rushed by and snatched feathers from birds to put on his cloak. The Indians were happy when he was gone because Hurakan made them afraid. Even today Hurakan comes back once in a while in the shape of a storm which people call a hurricane.

There was a day when the peaceful tribes who fished in the Gulf were driven away from their homes by fierce tribes from the north. Unlike the Indians who lived on the coast these tribes liked to kill. When they saw the birds flying around, they shot them with arrows. They caught them on their roosts at night. They robbed their nests. The poor birds cried out at the tops of their voices for the Storm God to save them.

Far off down in his home in the warm seas the god lifted his head and heard their cries. Quickly he rose to his feet and shook himself. Thunder broke loose over his head, so angry was he. He ran and jumped upon the back of Hurakan. He shouted for Hurakan to hurry. Shooting fire like lightning from his eyes and shaking loose black clouds from the tips of his great wings the Storm God's thunder bird flew toward the Texas coast. He and the god were wrapped in darkness, and as they flew across the sky the day became like night and the waters of the Gulf broke into white foam.

The Indians who were killing the birds saw the thunder god coming too late to get away. The sun was gone and the clouds were so thick that the day was like night. The wind from Hurakan's wings hit the Indians and blew them down when they tried to run. Behind them came the waters of the Gulf, pushed upon the land by the wind stirred up by the Storm God's thunder bird. The wind ` blew the birds high in the air, but it drove the water into the camps of the bad Indians and scattered their homes and made the Indians climb into trees. The Gulf now poured far inland over the prairie, and the prairie was like the sea.

Everywhere was rolling water, leaping waves, crying winds. High above the earth the Storm God rode his thunder bird and shouted with joy while the wind blew his long hair loose through the flying clouds.

At last, the god went away. As he left, the waters of the Gulf began to roll back from the land, and when they reached the ocean bed again, they dropped the mud and sand they had torn loose from the land and brought with them. The mud and sand began to pile up. Soon many islands were forming. They rose higher and higher as the waters kept dropping their loads of earth around them. When all was done the Texas coast was dotted with islands that were new homes for the birds. Indians could not reach those birds any longer. The pelicans, the gulls, the sand pipers and all the others now went to their new homes and made their nests where they could be safe and where the

Storm God could find them when he wanted new feathers for his cloak.

To this day those islands remain. Dwarf trees, cactus plants, weeds, grasses and flowers cover them like fairy gardens. And thousands of birds live on them, sing amid the bushes and bathe in the little pools left by the rains. During spring and summer, they lay their eggs and raise their little ones. They are happy and safe from men, because long ago the Storm God built the islands for them.

Qalagánguasê,
Who Passed to the Land of
Ghosts

Inuit

There was once a boy whose name was Qalagánguasê; his
parents lived at a place where the tides were strong. And
one day they ate seaweed, and died of it. Then there was
only one sister to look after Qalagánguasê, but it was not
long before she also died, and then there were only
strangers to look after him.

Qalagánguasê was without strength, the lower part of his
body was dead, and one day when the others had gone out
hunting, he was left alone in the house. He was sitting there
quite alone, when suddenly he heard a sound. Now he was
afraid, and with great pains he managed to drag himself out

of the house into the one beside it, and here he found a
hiding-place behind the skin hangings. And while he was in
hiding there, he heard a noise again, and in walked a ghost.

"Ai! There are people here!"

The ghost went over to the water tub and drank, emptying
the dipper twice.

"Thanks for the drink which I thirsty one received," said
the ghost. "Thus, I was wont to drink when I lived on
earth." And then it went out.

Now the boy heard his fellow-villagers coming up and
gathering outside the house, and then they began to crawl
in through the passage way.

"Qalagánguasê is not here," they said, when they came
inside.

"Yes, he is," said the boy. "I hid in here because a ghost
came in. It drank from the water tub there."

And when they went to look at the water tub, they saw that
something had been drinking from it.

Then some time after, it happened again that the people
were all out hunting, and Qalagánguasê alone in the place.
And there he sat in the house all alone, when suddenly the
walls and frame of the house began to shake, and next
moment a crowd of ghosts came tumbling into the house,
one after the other, and the last was one whom he knew, for
it was his sister, who had died but a little time before.

And now the ghosts sat about on the floor and began playing; they wrestled, and told stories, and laughed all the time.

At first Qalagánguasê was afraid of them, but at last he found it a pleasant thing to make the night pass. And not until the villagers could be heard returning did, they hasten away.

"Now mind you do not tell tales," Said the ghost, "for if you do as we say, then you will gain strength again, and there will be nothing you cannot do." And one by one they tumbled out of the passage way. Only Qalagánguasê's sister could hardly get out, and that was because her brother had been minding her little child, and his touch stayed her. And the hunters were coming back, and quite close, when she slipped out. One could just see the shadow of a pair of feet.

"What was that," said one. "It looked like a pair of feet vanishing away."

"Listen, and I will tell you," Said Qalagánguasê, who already felt his strength returning. "The house has been full of people, and they made the night pass pleasantly for me, and now, they say, I am to grow strong again."

But hardly had the boy said these words, when the strength slowly began to leave him.

"Qalagánguasê is to be challenged to a singing contest," he heard them say, as he lay there. And then they tied the boy to the frame post and let him swing backwards and forwards, as he tried to beat the drum. After that, they all made ready, and set out for their singing contest, and left the lame boy behind in the house all alone. And there he lay all alone, when his mother, who had died long since, came in with his father.

"Why are you here alone?" they asked.

"I am lame," said the boy, and when the others went off to a singing contest, they left me behind."

"Come away with us," said his father and mother.

"It is better so, perhaps," said the boy.

And so, they led him out, and bore him away to the land of ghosts, and so Qalagánguasê became a ghost.

And it is said that Qalagánguasê became a woman when they changed him to a ghost. But his fellow-villagers never saw him again.

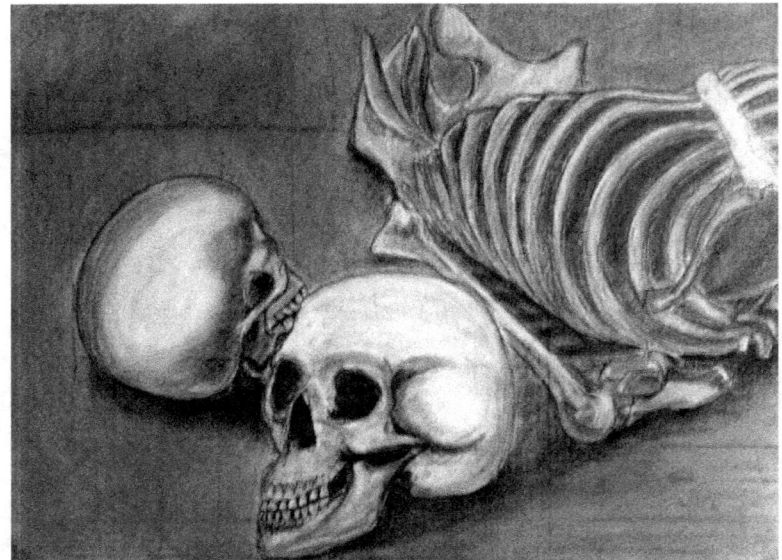

The Deserted Village

Seneca

A Grandfather and grandson lived together. They were the only persons left of a large nation. All their relatives and friends had been killed.

When the boy was old enough, his grandfather made him a bow and arrows and taught him to hunt. He killed small animals at first, but after a while he killed a deer. Each time he brought home game his grandfather danced and rejoiced, and mentioned the name of the game,

The two lived happily together till the grandson was a young man, then one day his grandfather said to him, "You are old enough to marry. I would like to have a woman here to cook. You must go South and find a wife. For an ordinary man it is a long journey but you will go quickly," and giving his grandson a pair of moccasins, he sent him off.

About midday the young man came to an opening in the woods. In the opening was a large village. He went from one house to another; all were empty. Then he went to the long house and looking in saw, on a bench, the body of a young woman. The corpse was ornamented with beautiful beads.

The young man thought, "I'll take some of those beads, they will be nice for my wife, when I find one."

He took what beads he wanted and when outside, said to himself, "I'll go home now and look for a wife some other time."

He started northward, as he thought, and ran along swiftly.

After a while he came to a clearing and to his surprise found it was the same one, he had left. Looking at the village and the long house, he thought, "I must have made a mistake."

He took bearings again and hurried toward home. Again, he came out in the village.

"It must be that woman brings me here because I have taken her beads. I'll give them back to her."

He went to the long house, put the beads on to the body, and again started for home. On the way he killed a bear and skinned it. Taking some of the meat he rolled it up in the skin, made a pack and carried it along, running as fast as he could, hoping to reach home before night.

At night he came out in the same opening.

"This is strange," thought he, "I'll have to spend the night in the long house."

He kindled a fire, cooked his meat, spread out the bear skin and sat down to eat. As he ate, he threw the bones behind him; soon he heard crunching and gnawing.

"Maybe a hungry ghost does that," thought he, "I'll give it some meat."

He threw pieces of meat behind him and heard them eaten.

After he had eaten enough, he crawled under the bear skin to sleep. Soon something began to pull the bear skin from his feet. He sprang up, stirred the fire and put on more wood. All was quiet, and he lay down again. After a while, when the fire had grown dim, something crawled over his body, came up to his breast. He threw his arms around the thing, wrapped it in the bearskin and sprang to his feet. A terrible struggle began.

The two wrestled from near the fire to the end of the long house and then down along the other side. When near the place they had started from, the gray of daylight came. That minute what seemed to be a body, dropped to the floor and lay still. The young man lashed the bearskin around it closely, left it on the floor and cooked and ate his breakfast.

He was curious to know what was in the skin, for he thought it must be something connected with the woman. Opening the skin carefully he found only a piece of clotted blood about the size of his fist.

He heated water, dissolved the blood, and, with a wooden ladle he whittled out with his flint knife, he poured some of the blood into the woman's mouth. It went down her throat. Again and again, he poured. At last, the woman's breast began to move. When he had given her half the blood she breathed.

When she had taken it all, she said, "I am hungry."

The young man pounded corn, made thin gruel and fed her. Soon she was able to sit up and in a little while she was well.

She said, "People lived in this village till a short time ago. Many men from the North have wanted to marry me, when I was unwilling and refused each one of them, they changed me and drove my father and all his people away. I was left here for dead."

"Come," said the young man, "We will go and find your father."

They set out together, and after a while came to a village. Crow, with his large family, lived in the house at the edge of the village. When the young man told Crow the story of the long house and the chief's daughter, Crow said, "My chief is this girl's father. I'll tell him that his daughter is alive."

Crow hurried to the chief's house and said to the chief, "Your daughter is alive."

The mother screamed, "You lie! no one ever came to life after being dead more than ten days." And taking up a club she started to drive Crow out of the house.

"Don't strike him," said the chief, "Maybe our daughter has come to life."

"She has," said Crow, "She is in my house now.

"Tell her to come here," said the chief.

When the chief and his wife saw their daughter, they were happy, and, as they were willing, the young man became their son-in-law.

After a few days the man said to his wife, "Borrow your father's bow and arrows, all the young men in the village are to hunt to-morrow; I must go with them."

Each man went alone, starting early. Crow met the young man, and said, "I'll fly high and look around, see where the deer are."

Crow saw ten deer some distance away. He came down and said, "I'll fly behind those deer and drive them toward you, you can kill them."

The! young man waited till the deer passed, then when all were in line, he killed the ten with one arrow.

Crow said, "The hunters never give me anything but intestines."

"You may have a whole deer to-day," said the young man. Crow flew home with the news, and asked, "What are our young men good for? The chief's son-in-law has killed ten deer before sunrise."

The other hunters had bad luck.

At night there was a feast and a dance in the long house.

The hunters planned to kill the young man. When in the dance he came to the middle of the long house, by their magic they made him sink deep into the ground, disappear. But Crow knew where he was, and when all were gone, he called upon his friend Turkey to dig up the young man.

Turkey came and scratched till at last he had the dirt away, then Crow made a rope and together they drew the young man out of the ground.

The chief decided to leave the enemies of his son-in-law and go with the good people, the friends of his son-in-law, to live in the village where the young man's grandfather lived.

They went there, settled down, and lived happily.

The Boy from the Bottom of the Sea, Who Frightened the People of the House to Death

Inuit

Well, you see it was the usual thing: "The Obstinate One" had taken a wife, and of course he beat her, and when he wanted to make it an extra special beating, he took a box, and banged her about with that.

One day, when he had been beating her as usual, she ran away. And she was just about to have a child at that time. She walked straight out into the sea, and was nearly drowned, but suddenly she came to herself again, and found that she was at the bottom of the sea. And there she built herself a house.

While she was down there, the child was born. And when she went to look at it, she nearly died of fright, it was so ugly. Its eyes were jellyfish, its hair of seaweed, and the mouth was like a mussel.

And now these two lived down there together. The child grew up, and when it was a little grown up, it could hear the children playing on the earth up above, and it said:

"I should like to go up and see."

"When you have grown stronger, then you may go," said his mother. And then the boy began practicing feats of strength, with stones. And at last, he was able to pick up stones as big as a chest, and carry them into the house.

One evening, when it was dark, they heard again a calling from above. The children, not content with simply shouting at their play, began crying out: "*Iyoi-iyoi-iyoi*," with all their might.

"Now I will go with you," said the mother. "But you must not go into the houses nearest the shore, for there I often fled in when your father would have beaten me; I have suffered much evil up there. And when you thrust in your head, be sure to look as angry as you can."

There were two houses on the shore, one a little way above the other. As they went up, the mother suddenly saw that her son was going into the one nearest the shore. And she cried:

"Ha-a; Ha-a! When your father beat me, I always ran in there. Go to the one up above."

And now the boy made his face fierce, and thrust in his head at the doorway, and all those inside fell down dead with fright. He would have beaten his father, but his father had died long since. Then he went down again to the bottom of the sea.

When the day dawned, the people from the house nearest the shore came out and said:

"Ai! What footsteps are these, all full of seaweed?"

And seeing that the tracks led up to the house a little way above, they followed there, and found that all inside had died of fright.

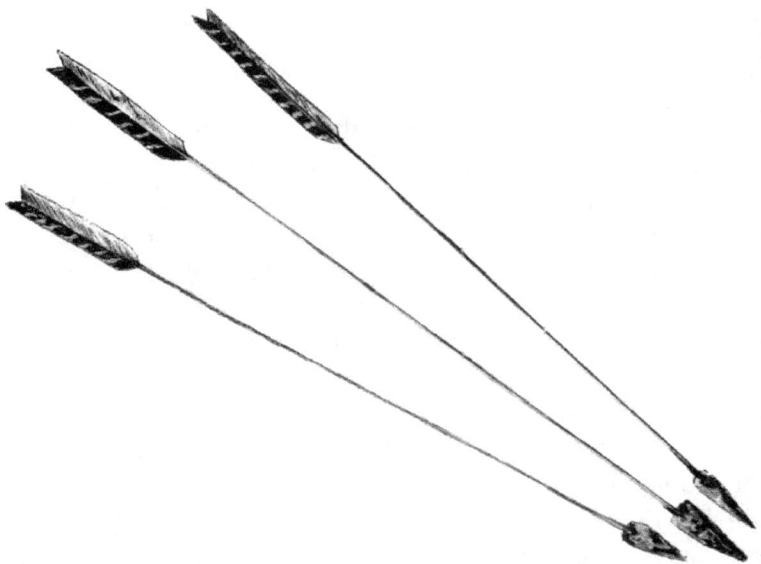

The Water Cannibals

Cherokee

Besides the friendly Nûñnë'hï of the streams and mountains there is a race of cannibal spirits, who stay at the bottom of the deep rivers and live upon human flesh, especially that of little children. They come out just after daybreak and go about unseen from house to house until they find some one still asleep, when they shoot him with their invisible arrows and carry the dead body down under the water to feast upon it. That no one may know what has happened they leave in place of the body a shade or image of the dead man or little child, that wakes up and talks and goes about just as he did, but there is no life in it, and in seven days it withers and dies, and the people bury it and think they are burying their dead friend. It was a long time before the people found out about this, but now they always try to be awake at daylight and wake up the children, telling them "The hunters are among you."

This is the way they first knew about the water cannibals: There was a man in Tïkwäli'tsï town who became sick and grew worse until the doctors said he could not live, and then his friends went away from the house and left him alone to die. They were not so kind to each other in the old times as they are now, because they were afraid of the witches that came to torment dying people.

He was alone several days, not able to rise from his bed, when one morning an old woman came in at the door. She looked just like the other women of the settlement, but he did not know her. She came over to the bed and said, "You are very sick and your friends seem to have left you. Come with me and I will make you well." The man was so near death that he could not move, but now her words made him feel stronger at once, and he asked her where she wanted him to go. "We live close by; come with me and I will show you," said the woman, so he got up from his bed and she led the way down to the water. When she came to the water she stepped in and he followed, and there was a road under the water, and another country there just like that above.

They went on until they came to a settlement with a great many houses, and women going about their work and children playing. They met a party of hunters coming in from a hunt, but instead of deer or bear quarters hanging from their shoulders they carried the bodies of dead men and children, and several of the bodies the man knew for those of his own friends in Tïkwäli'tsï. They came to a house and the woman said "This is where I live," and took him in and fixed a bed for him and made him comfortable.

By this time, he was very hungry, but the woman knew his thoughts and said, "We must get him something to eat. She took one of the bodies that the hunters had just brought in and cut off a slice to roast. The man was terribly frightened, but she read his thoughts again and said, "I see you can not eat our food." Then she turned away from him and held her hands before her stomach--*so*--and when she turned around again, she had them full of bread and beans such as he used to have at home.

So, it was every day, until soon he was well and strong again. Then she told him he might go home now, but he must be sure not to speak to anyone for seven days, and if any of his friends should question him, he must make signs as if his throat were sore and keep silent. She went with him along the same trail to the water's edge, and the water closed over her and he went back alone to Tïkwäli'tsï. When he came there his friends were surprised, because they thought he had wandered off and died in the woods. They asked him where he had been, but he only pointed to his throat and said nothing, so they thought he was not yet well and let him alone until the seven days were past, when he began to talk again and told the whole story.

Átahsaia, the Cannibal Demon

Zuñi

In the days of the ancients, when the children of our forefathers lived in Héshokta (" Town of the Cliffs '), there also lived two beautiful maidens, elder and younger, sisters one to the other, daughters of a master-chief.

One bright morning in summer-time, the elder sister called to the younger, "*Háni!*"

"What sayest thou?" said the *háni*.

"The day is bright and the water is warm. Let us go down to the pool and wash our clothes, that we may wear them as if new at the dance to come."

"Ah, yes, sister elder," said the *háni*; "but these are days when they say the shadows of the rocks and even the sage-bushes lodge unthinkable things, and cause those who walk alone to breathe hard with fear."

"*Shtchu!*" exclaimed the elder sister derisively. "Younger sisters always are as timid as younger brothers are bad-tempered."

"Ah, well, then; as you will, sister elder. I will not quarrel with your wish, but I fear to go."

"*Yaush!* Come along, then," said the elder sister; whereupon they gathered their cotton mantles and other garments into bundles, and, taking along a bag of yucca-root, or soap-weed, started together down the steep, crooked path to where the pool lay at the foot of the great mesa.

Now, far above the Town of the Cliffs, among the rocks of red-gray and yellow--red in the form of a bowlder-like mountain that looks like a frozen sand-bank--there is a deep cave. You have never seen it? Well! to this day it is called the "Cave of Átahsaia," and there, in the times I tell of, lived Átahsaia himself. Uhh! what an ugly demon he was! His body was as big as the biggest elks, and his breast was shaggy with hair as stiff as porcupine-quills. His legs and arms were long and brawny, --all covered with speckled scales of black and white. His hair was coarse and snarly as a buffalo's mane, and his eyes were so big and glaring that they popped out of his head like skinned onions.

His mouth stretched from one cheek to the other and was filled with crooked fangs as yellow as thrown-away deer-bones. His lips were as red and puffy as peppers, and his face as wrinkled and rough as a piece of burnt buckskin. That was Átahsaia, who in the days of the ancients, devoured men and women for his meat, and the children of men for his sweet-bread. His weapons were terrible, too. His finger-nails were as long as the claws of a bear, and in his left hand he carried a bow made of the sapling of a mountain-oak, with two arrows ready drawn for use. And he was never seen without his great flint knife, as broad as a man's thigh and twice as long, which he brandished with his right hand and poked his hair back with, so that his grizzly fore-locks were covered with the blood of those he had slaughtered. He wore over his shoulders, whole skins of the mountain lion and bear clasped with buttons of wood.

Now, although Átahsaia was ugly and could not speak without chattering his teeth, or laugh without barking like a wolf, he was a very polite demon. But, like many ugly and polite people nowadays, he was a great liar.

Átahsaia that morning woke up and stuck his head out of his hole just as the two maidens went down to the spring. He caught sight of them while his eyes travelled below, and he chuckled. Then he muttered, as he gazed at them and saw how young and fine, they were: "*Ahhali! Yaatchi!*" (" Good lunch! Two for a munch!") and howled his war-cry, "Ho-o-o-thlai-a!" till Teshaminkia, the Echo-God, shouted it to the maidens.

"Oh!" exclaimed the háni, clutching the arm of her elder sister; "listen!"

"*Ho-o-o-thlai-a!*" again roared the demon, and again Teshaminkia.

"Oh, oh! sister elder, what did I tell you

"Why did we come out today!" and both ran away; then stopped to listen. When they heard nothing more, they returned to the spring and went to washing their clothes on some flat stones.

But Átahsaia grabbed up his weapons and began to clamber down the mountain. muttering and chuckling to himself as he went: "*Ahhali! Yaatchi!*" (" Good lunch! Two for a munch!").

Around the corner of Great Mesa, on the high shelves of
which stands the Town of the Cliffs, are two towering
buttes called Kwilli-yallon (Twin Mountain). Far up on the
top of this mountain there dwelt Áhaiyúta and Mátsailéma.

You don't know who Áhaiyúta and Mátsailéma were? Well,
I will tell you. They were the twin children of the Sun-
father and the Mother Waters of the World. Before men
were born to the light, the Sun made love to the Waters of
the World, and under his warm, bright glances, there were
hatched out of a foam-cup on the face of the Great Ocean,
which then covered the earth, two wonderful boys, whom
men afterward named *Ua nam Atch Píahk'oa* ("The
Beloved Two Who Fell"). The Sun dried away the waters
from the high-lands of earth and these Two then delivered
men forth from the bowels of our Earth-mother, and guided
them eastward toward the home of their father, the Sun.
The time came, alas! when war and many strange beings
arose to destroy the children of earth, and then the eight
Stern Beings changed the hearts of the twins to *sawanikia*,
or the medicine of war. Thenceforth they were known as
Áhaiyúta and Mátsailéma ("Our Beloved," the "Terrible
Two," "Boy-gods of War").

Even though changed, they still guarded our ancients and
guided them to the Middle of the World, where we now
live. Gifted with hearts of the medicine of war, and with
wisdom almost as great as the Sun-father's own, they
became the invincible guardians of the Corn-people of
Earth, and, with the rainbow for their weapon and
thunderbolts for their arrows, --swift lightning-shafts
pointed with turquoise, --were the greatest warriors of all in
the days of the new. When at last they had conquered most
of the enemies of men, they taught to chosen few of their
followers the songs, prayers, and orders of a society of
warriors who should be called their children, the Priests of

the Bow, and selecting from among them the two wisest, breathed into their nostrils (as they have since breathed into those of their successors) the *sawanikia*. Since then, we make anew the semblance of their being and place them each year at midsun on the top of the Mountain of Thunder, and on the top of the Mountain of the Beloved, that they may know we remember them and that they may guard (as it was said in the days of the ancients they would guard) the Land of Zuñi from sunrise to sunset and cut off the pathways of the enemy.

Well, Áhaiyúta, who is called the elder brother, and Mátsailéma, who is called the younger, were living on the top of Twin Mountain with their old grandmother.

Said the elder to the younger on this same morning: "Brother, let us go out and hunt. It is a fine day. What say you?

"My face is in front of me," said the younger, "and under a roof is no place for men," he added, as he put on his helmet of elk-hide and took a quiver of mountain-lion skin from an antler near the ladder.

"Where are you two boys going now?" shrieked the grandmother through a trap-door from below.

Don't you ever intend to stop worrying me by going abroad when even the spaces breed fear like thick war?"

"O grandmother," they laughed, as they tightened their bows and straightened their arrows before the fire, "never mind us; we are only going out for a hunt," and before the old woman could climb up to stop them, they were gaily skipping down the rocks toward the cliffs below.

Suddenly the younger brother stopped. "Ahh!" said he,
"listen, brother! It is the cry of Átahsaia, and the old wretch
is surely abroad to cause tears!"

"Yes," replied the elder. "It is Átahsaia, and we must stop
him! Come on, come on; quick!"

"Hold, brother, hold! Stiffen your feet right here with
patience. He is after the two maidens of Héshokta! I saw
them going to the spring as I came down. This day he must
die. Is your face to the front?"

"It is; come on," said the elder brother, starting forward.

"Stiffen your feet with patience, I say," again exclaimed the
younger brother. "Know you that the old demon comes up
the pathway below here? He will not hurt them until he gets
them home. You know he is a great liar, and a great
flatterer; that is the way the old beast catches people. Now,
if we wait here, we will surely see them when they come
up."

So, after quarrelling a little, the elder brother consented to
sit down on a rock which overlooked the pathway and was
within bow-shot of the old demon's cave.

Now, while the girls were washing, Átahsaia ran as fast as
his old joints would let him until the two girls heard his
mutterings and rattling weapons.

"Something is coming, sister!" cried the younger, and both
ran toward the rocks to hide again, but they were too late.
The old demon strode around by another way and suddenly,
at a turn, came face to face with them, glaring with his
bloodshot eyes and waving his great jagged flint knife. But
as he neared them, he lowered the knife and smiled,

straightening himself up and approaching the frightened ones as gently as would a young man.

The poor younger sister clung to the elder one, and sank moaning by her side, for the smile of Átahsaia was as fearful as the scowl of a triumphant enemy, or the laugh of a rattlesnake when he hears any old man tell a lie and thinks he will poison him for it.

"Why do you run, and why do you weep so? asked the old demon. "I know you. I am ugly and old, my pretty maidens, but I am your grandfather and mean you no harm at all. I frightened you only because I felt certain you would run away from me if you could."

"Ah!" faltered the elder sister, immediately getting over her fright. "We did not know you and therefore we were frightened by you. Come, sister, come," said she to the younger. "Brighten your eyes and thoughts, for our grandfather will not hurt us. Don't you see?"

But the younger sister only shook her head and sobbed. Then the demon got angry. "What are you blubbering about?" he roared, raising his knife and sweeping it wildly through the air. "Do you see this knife? This day I will cut off the light of your life with it if you do not swallow your whimpers!"

"Get up, oh, do get up, *háni!*" whispered the elder sister, now again frightened herself. "Surely he will not cut us off just now, if we obey him; and is it not well that even for a little time the light of life shine-though it shine through fear and sadness-than be cut off altogether? For who knows where the trails tend that lead through the darkness of the night of death?"

You know, in the speech of the rulers of the world and of our ancients, a man's light was cut off when his life was taken, and when he died, he came to the dividing-place of life.

The *háni* tried to rally herself and rose to her feet, but she still trembled.

"Now, my pretty maidens, my own granddaughters, even," said the old demon once more, as gently as at first, "I am most glad I found you. How good are the gods! for I am a poor, lone old man. All my people are gone." (Here he sighed like the hiss of a wild-cat.) "Yonder above is my home" (pointing over his shoulder), 'and as I am a great hunter, plenty of venison is baking in my rear room and more sweet-bread than I can eat. Lo! it makes me homesick to eat alone, and when I saw you and saw how pretty and gentle you were, I thought that it might be you would throw the light of your favor on me, and go up to my house to share of my abundance and drink from my vessels. Besides, I am so old that only now and then can I get a full jar of water up to my house. So, I came as fast as I could to ask you to return and eat with me."

Reassured by his kind speech, the elder sister hastened to say: "Of course, we will go with our grandfather, and if that is all he may want of us, we can soon fill his water-jars, can't we, *háni?*"

"You are a good girl," said the old demon to the one who had spoken; then, glaring at the younger sister: "Bring that fool along with you and come up; she will not come by herself; she has more bashfulness than sense, and less sense than my knife, because that makes the world more wise by killing off fools."

He led the way and the elder sister followed, dragging along the shrinking *háni*.

The old demon kept talking in a loud voice as they went up the pathway, telling all sorts of entertaining stories, until, as they neared the rocks where Áhaiyúta and Mátsailéma were waiting, the Two heard him and said to one another: "Ahh, they come!"

Then the elder brother jumped up and began to tighten his bow, but the younger brother muttered: "Sit down, won't you, you fool! Átahsaia's ears are like bat-ears, only bigger. Wait now, till I say ready. You know he will not hurt the girls until he gets them out from his house. Look over there in front of his hole. Do you see the flat place that leads along to that deep chasm beyond?"

"Yes," replied the elder brother. "But what of that?"

"What but that there he cuts the throats of his captives and casts their bones and heads into the depths of the chasm! Do you see the notch in the stone? That's where he lets their blood flow down, and for that reason no one ever discovers his tracks. Now, stiffen your feet with patience, I say, and we will see what to do when the time comes.

Again, they sat and waited. As the old demon and the girls passed along below, the elder brother again started and would have shot had not Mátsailéma held him back. "You fool of a brother elder, but not wiser, No! Do you not know that your arrow is lightning and will kill the maidens as well as the monster?"

Finally, the demon reached the entrance to his cave, and, going in, asked the girls to follow him, laying out two slabs for them to sit on. "Now, sit down, my pretty girls, and I will soon get something for you to eat. You must be hungry." Going to the rear of the cave, he broke open a stone oven, and the steam which arose was certainly delicious and meaty. Soon he brought out two great bowls, big enough to feed a whole dance. One contained meat, the other a mess resembling sweet-bread pudding. "Now, let us eat," said the demon, seating himself opposite, and at once diving his horny fingers and scaly hand half up to the wrist in the meat-broth. The elder sister began to take bits of the food to eat it, when the younger made a motion to her, and showed her with horror the bones of a little hand. The sweet-bread was the flesh and bones of little children. Then the two girls only pretended to eat, taking the food out and throwing it down by the side of the bowls.

"Why don't you eat?" demanded the demon, cramming at the same time a huge mouthful of the meat, bones and all, into his wide throat.

"We are eating," said one of the girls.

"Then why do you throw my food away?"

"We are throwing away only the bones."

"Well, the bones are the better part," retorted the demon, taking another huge mouthful, by way of example, big enough to make a grown man's meal. "Oh, yes!" he added; "I forgot that you had baby teeth."

After the meal was finished, the old demon said: "Let us go out and sit down in the sun on my terrace. Perhaps, my pretty maidens, you will comb an old man's hair, for I have no one left to help me now," he sighed, pretending to be very sad. So, showing the girls where to sit down, without waiting for their assent he settled himself in front of them and leaned his head back to have it combed. The two maidens dared not disobey; and now and then they pulled at a long, coarse hair, and then snapped their fingers close to his scalp, which so deceived the old demon that he grunted with satisfaction every time. At last, their knees were so tired by his weight upon them that they said they were done, and Átahsaia, rising, pretended to be greatly pleased, and thanked them over and over. Then he told them to sit down in front of him, and he would comb their hair as they had combed his, but not to mind if he hurt a little for his fingers were old and stiff. The two girls again dared not disobey, and sat down as he had directed. Uhh! how the old beast grinned and glared and breathed softly between his teeth.

The two brothers had carefully watched everything, the elder one starting up now and then, the younger remaining quiet. Suddenly Mátsailéma sprang up. He caught the shield the Sun-father had given him, --the shield which, though made only of nets and knotted cords, would ward off alike the weapons of the warrior or the magic of the wizard. Holding it aloft, he cried to Áhaiyúta: "Stand ready; the time is come! If I miss him, pierce him with your arrow. Now, then--"

He hurled the shield through the air. Swiftly as a hawk and noiselessly as an owl, it sailed straight over the heads of the maidens and settled between them and the demon's face. The shield was invisible, and the old demon knew not it was there. He leaned over as if to examine the maidens' heads. He opened his great mouth, and, bending yet nearer, made a vicious bite at the elder one.

"Ai, ai! my poor little sister, alas!" with which both fell to sobbing and moaning, and crouched, expecting instantly to be destroyed. But the demon's teeth caught in the meshes of the invisible shield, and, howling with vexation, he began struggling to free himself of the encumbrance. Áhaiyúta drew a shaft to the point and let fly. With a thundering noise that rent the rocks, and a rush of strong wind, the shaft blazed through the air and buried itself in the demon's shoulders, piercing him through ere the thunder had half done pealing. Swift as mountain sheep were the leaps and light steps of the brothers, who, bounding to the shelf of rock, drew their war-clubs and soon softened the hard skull of the old demon with them. The younger sister was unharmed save by fright; but the elder sister lay where she had sat, insensible.

"Hold!" cried Mátsailéma, "she was to blame, but then-" Lifting the swooning maiden in his strong little arms, he laid her apart from the others, and, breathing into her nostrils, soon revived her eyes to wisdom.

"This day have we, through the power of sawanikia, seen for our father an enemy of our children, men. A beast that caused unto fatherless children, unto men less women, unto womenless men (who thus became through his evil will), tears and sad thoughts, has this day been looked upon by the Suit and laid low. May the favors of the gods thus meet us ever."

Thus said the two brothers, as they stood over the gasping, still struggling but dying demon; and as they closed their little prayer, the maidens, who now first saw whom they had to thank for their deliverance, were overwhelmed with gladness, yet shame. They exclaimed, in response to the prayer: *"May they, indeed, thus meet you and ourselves!"*

Then they breathed upon their hands.

The two brothers now turned toward the girls. "Look ye upon the last enemy of men," said they, "whom this day we have had the power of *sawanikia* given us to destroy; whom this day the father of all, our father the Sun, has looked upon, whose light of life this day our weapons have cut off; whose path of life this day our father has divided. Not ourselves, but our father has done this deed, through us. Haste to your home in Héshokta and tell your father these things; and tell him, pray, that he must assemble his priests and teach them these our words, for we divide our paths of life henceforth from one another and from the paths of men, no more to mingle save in spirit with the children of men. But we shall depart for our everlasting home in the mountains--the one to the Mountain of Thunder, the other to the Mount of the Beloved--to guard from sunrise to sunset the land of the Corn-priests of Earth, that the foolish among men break not into the Middle Country of Earth and lay it waste. Yet we shall require of our children the plumes wherewith we dress our thoughts, and the forms of our being wherewith men may renew us each year at midsun. Henceforth two stars at morning and evening will be seen, the one going before, the other following, the Sun-father--the one Áhaiyúta, his herald; the other Mátsailéma, his guardian; warriors both, and fathers of men. May the trail of life be finished ere divided! Go ye happily hence."

The maidens breathed from the hands of the Twain, and with bowed heads and a prayer of thanks started down the pathway toward the Town of the Cliffs. When they came to their home, the old father asked whence they came. They told the story of their adventure and repeated the words of the Beloved.

The old man bowed his head, and said: "It was Áhaiyúta and Mátsailéma!" Then he made a prayer of thanks, and

cast abroad on the wind's white meal of the seeds of earth
and shells from the Great Waters of the World, the pollen
of beautiful flowers, and the paints of war.

"It is well!" he said. "Four days hence I will assemble my
warriors, and we will cut the plume-sticks, paint and
feather them, and place them on high mountains, that
through their knowledge and power of medicine our
Beloved Two Warriors may take them unto themselves."

Now, when the maidens disappeared among the rocks
below, the brothers looked each at the other and laughed.
Then they shouted, and Áhaiyúta kicked Átahsaia's ugly
carcass till it gurgled, at which the two boys shouted again
most hilariously and laughed. "That's what we proposed to
do with you, old beast!" they cried out.

"But, brother younger," said Áhaiyúta, "what shall be done
with him now?"

"Let's skin him," said Mátsailéma.

So, they set to work and skinned the body from foot to
head, as one skins a fawn when one wishes to make a seed-
bag. Then they put sticks into the legs and arms, and tied
strings to them, and stuffed the body with dry grass and
moss; and where they set the thing up against the cliff it
looked verily like the living Átahsaia.

"Uhh! what an ugly beast he was!" said Mátsailéma. Then
he shouted: "*Wahaha, hihiho!*" and almost doubled up with
laughter. "Won't we have fun with old grandmother,
though. Hurry up; let's take care of the rest of him!"

They cut off the head, and Áhaiyúta said to it: "*Thou hast
been a liar, and told a falsehood for every life thou hast*

taken in the world; therefore, shall thou become a lying star, and each night thy guilt shall be seen of all men throughout the wide world." He twirled the bloody head around once or twice, and cast it with all might into the air. *Wa muu!* it sped through the spaces into the middle of the sky like a spirt of blood, and now it is a great red star. It rises in summer-time and tells of the coming morning when it is only midnight; hence it is called *Mokwanosana* (Great Lying Star).

Then Mátsailéma seized the great knife and ripped open the abdomen with one stroke. Grasping the intestines, he tore them out and exclaimed: "*Ye have devoured and digested the flesh of men over the whole wide world; therefore, ye shall be stretched from one end of the earth to the other, and the children of those ye have wasted will look upon ye every night and will say to one another:*

'Ah, the entrails of him who caused sad thoughts to our grandfathers shine well tonight!' and they will laugh and sneer at ye." Whereupon he slung the whole mass aloft, and *tsolo!* it stretched from one end of the world to the other, and became the Great Snow-drift of the Skies (Milky Way). Lifting the rest of the carcass, they threw it down into the chasm whither the old demon had thrown so many of his victims, and the rattlesnakes came out and ate of the flesh day after day till their fangs grew yellow with putrid meat, and even now their children's fangs are yellow and poisonous.

"Now, then, for some fun!" shouted Mátsailéma. Do you catch the old bag up and prance around with it a little; and I will run off to see how it looks."

Áhaiyúta caught up the effigy, and, hiding himself behind, pulled at the strings till it looked, of all things thinkable, like the living Átahsaia himself starting out for a hunt, for they threw the lion skins over it and tied the bow in its hand.

"Excellent! Excellent!" exclaimed the boys, and they clapped their hands and *wa-ha-ha-ed* and *ho-ho-ho-ed* till they were sore. Then, dragging the skin along, they ran as fast as they could, down to the plain below Twin Mountain.

The Sun was climbing down the western ladder, and their old grandmother had been looking all over the mountains and valleys below to see if the two boys were coming. She had just climbed the ladder and was gazing and fretting and saying: "Oh! those two boys! terrible pests and as hardhearted and as long-winded in having their own way as a turtle is in having his! Now, something has happened to them; I knew it would," when suddenly a frightened scream came up from below.

"*Ho-o-o-ta! Ho-o-o-ta!* Come quick! Help! Help!" the voice cried, as if in anguish.

"Uhh!" exclaimed the old woman, and she went so fast in her excitement that she tumbled through the trap-door, and then jumped up, scolding and groaning.

She grabbed a poker of piñon, and rushed out of the house. Sure enough, there was poor Mátsailéma running hard and calling again and again for her to hurry down. The old woman hobbled along over the rough path as fast as she could, and until her wind was blowing shorter and shorter, when, suddenly turning around the crags, she caught sight of Áhaiyúta struggling to get away from Átahsaia.

"*O ai o!* I knew it! I knew it!" cried the old woman; and she ran faster than ever until she came near enough to see that

101

her poor grandson was almost tired out, and that Mátsailéma had lost even his war-club. "Stiffen your feet, --my boys, --wait--a bit," puffed the old woman, and, flying into a passion, she rushed at the effigy and began to pound it with her poker, till the dust fairly smoked out of the dry grass, and the skin doubled up as if it were in pain.

Mátsailéma rolled and kicked in the grass, and Áhaiyúta soon had to let the stuffed demon fall down for sheer laughing. But the old woman never ceased. She belabored the demon and cursed his cannibal heart and told him that was what he got for chasing her grandsons, and that, and this, and that, whack! whack! without stopping, until she thought the monster surely must be dead. Then she was about to rest when suddenly the boys pulled the strings, and the demon sprang up before her, seemingly as well as ever. Again, the old woman fell to, but her strokes kept getting feebler and feebler, her breath shorter and shorter, until her wind went out and she fell to the ground.

How the boys did laugh and roll on the ground when the old grandmother moaned: "Alas! alas! This day--my day--light is--cut off--and my wind of life--fast going."

The old woman covered her head with her tattered mantle; but when she found that Átahsaia did not move, she raised her eyes and looked through a rent. There were her two grandsons rolling and kicking on the grass and holding their mouths with both hands, their eyes swollen and faces red with laughter. Then she suddenly looked for the demon. There lay the skin, all torn and battered out of shape.

"So, ho! you pesky wretches; that's the way you treat me, is it? Well! never again will I help you, never!" she snapped, "nor shall you ever live with me more!" Whereupon the old woman jumped up and hobbled away. But little did the brothers care. They laughed till she was far away, and then said one to the other: "It is done!"

Since that time, the grandmother has gone, no one knows where. But Áhaiyúta and Mátsailéma are the bright stars of the morning and evening, just in front of and behind the Sun-father himself. Yet their spirits hover over their shrines on Thunder Mountain and the Mount of the Beloved, they say, or linger over the Middle of the World, forever to guide the games and to guard the warriors of the Land of Zuñi. Thus, it was in the days of the ancients.

Thus shortens my story.

The Twelve Stars

Seneca

Twelve children were playing together on the grass near their fathers' cabins. They thought they would play a new game, and they invented one. They joined hands in a circle and danced, not swinging around, but standing in one place. As they danced, they sang: "We are dancing. We are dancing."

Their parents were watching them and listening to their song, when all at once they noticed that their feet did not touch the ground. The parents were frightened and ran out to stop the dancing, but the children were already above their heads in the air and going higher and higher, always singing: "We are dancing. We are dancing."

They went up and up until they disappeared, still holding hands, and they were next seen as twelve stars in the heavens just above their fathers' cabins. One got a little out of the circle and therefore appears a little at one side of the others.

The Man Who Married the Thunder's Sister

Cherokee

In the old times the people used to dance often and all night. Once there was a dance at the old town of Sâkwi'yï, on the head of Chattahoochee, and after it was well started two young women with beautiful long hair came in, but no one knew who they were, or whence they had come. They danced with one partner and another, and in the morning slipped away before anyone knew that they were gone; but a young warrior had fallen in love with one of the sisters on account of her beautiful hair, and after the manner of the Cherokee had already asked her through an old man if she would marry him and let him live with her. To this the young woman had replied that her brother at home must first be consulted, and they promised to return for the next dance seven days later with an answer, but in the meantime if the young man really loved her, he must prove his constancy by a rigid fast until then. The eager lover readily agreed and impatiently counted the days.

In seven nights, there was another dance. The young warrior was on hand early, and later in the evening the two sisters appeared as suddenly as before. They told him their brother was willing, and after the dance they would conduct the young man to their home, but warned him that if he told anyone where he went or what he saw he would surely die.

He danced with them again and about daylight the three came away just before the dance closed, so as to avoid being followed, and started off together. The women led the way along a trail through the woods, which the young man had never noticed before, until they came to a small creek, where, without hesitating, they stepped into the water. The young man paused in surprise on the bank and thought to himself, "They are walking in the water; I don't want to do that." The women knew his thoughts just as though he had spoken and turned and said to him, "This is not water; this is the road to our house." He still hesitated, but they urged him on until he stepped into the water and found it was only soft grass that made a fine level trail.

They went on until the trail came to a large stream which he knew for Tallulah River. The women plunged boldly in, but again the warrior hesitated on the bank, thinking to himself, "That water is very deep and will drown me; I can't go on." They knew his thoughts and turned and said, "This is no water, but the main trail that goes past our house, which is now close by." He stepped in, and instead of water there was tall waving grass that closed above his head as he followed them.

They went only a short distance and came to a rock cave close under Ugûñ'yï (Tallulah falls). The women. entered, while the warrior stopped at the mouth; but they said: "This is our house; come in and our brother will soon be home; he is coming now." They heard low thunder in the distance.

He went inside and stood tip close to the entrance. Then the women took off their long hair and hung it up on a rock, and both their heads were as smooth as a pumpkin. The man thought, "It is not hair at all," and he was more frightened than ever.

The younger woman, the one he was about to marry, then sat down and told him to take a seat beside her. He looked, and it was a large turtle, which raised itself up and stretched out its claws as if angry at being disturbed. The young man said it was a turtle, and refused to sit down, but the woman insisted that it was a seat. Then there was a louder roll of thunder and the woman said, "Now our brother is nearly home." While they urged and he still refused to come nearer or sit down, suddenly there was a great thunder clap just behind him, and turning quickly he saw a man standing in the doorway of the cave.

"This is my brother," said the woman, and he came in and sat down upon the turtle, which again rose up and stretched out its claws. The young warrior still refused to come in. The brother then said that he was just about to start to a council, and invited the young man to go with him. The hunter said he was willing to go if only he had a horse; so, the young woman was told to bring one. She went out and soon came back leading a great uktena snake, that curled and twisted along the whole length of the cave. Some people say this was a white uktena and that the brother himself rode a red one. The hunter was terribly frightened, and said "That is a snake; I can't ride that." The others insisted that it was no snake, but their riding horse. The brother grew impatient and said to the woman, "He may like it better if you bring him a saddle, and some bracelets for his wrists and arms." So, they went out again and brought in a saddle and some arm bands, and the saddle was another turtle, which they fastened on the uktena's back, and the bracelets were living slimy snakes, which they got ready to twist around the hunter's wrists.

He was almost dead with fear, and said, "What kind of horrible place is this? I can never stay here to live with snakes and creeping things." The brother got very angry and called him a coward, and then it was as if lightening flashed from his eyes and struck the young man, and a terrible crash of thunder stretched him senseless.

When at last he came to himself again he was standing with his feet in the water and both hands grasping a laurel bush that grew out from the bank, and there was no trace of the cave or the Thunder People, but he was alone in the forest. He made his way out and finally reached his own settlement, but found then that he had been gone so very long that all the people had thought him dead, although to him it seemed only the day after the dance. His friends questioned him closely, and, forgetting the warning, he told the story; but in seven days he died, for no one can come back from the underworld and tell it and live.

The Maiden Who Loved a Star

Tejas

There was once a young and beautiful Indian girl who went from her home into a desert of the western country to gather there the purple ripe fruit of the prickly pear. She left the desert late one day after the sun had gone down, and when she set out for home the bright stars were beginning to sparkle in the sky. One star was much brighter than the others, and seemed closer to earth than the others. The Indian maiden stopped in the sand and watched it. Was the star winking down at her? She thought it was. She dreamed of the shining star that night, and she saw in her dream that the star was the home of a fine, tall youth, a sky dweller.

The next day the maiden went again into the desert to gather the fruit of the prickly pear. Again, she stayed until the sun had gone down behind the distant hills on the far edge of the desert, and she watched her star winking once more at her. That was the sky youth, she knew. For seven days she visited the desert and each night she dreamed of this fair young man. She dreamed that he spoke of his love to her, but he could not join her on earth as long as she lived there and as long as he lived in the sky. He could not come down to the desert. She could not visit him in his star home.

The maiden was full of love, but she was unhappy because she was so far away from her lover in the star-frosted sky. She decided she did not want to live any longer. An old witch woman lived with the tribe, and the Indian maiden went to her and asked the woman how to die in order that she might be taken up to the sky to live in the star with her lover.

"Life is too great a gift to be flung aside," said the witch woman as she looked at the poor girl weeping on the other side of the old woman's fire. "You must live out the life the Great Spirit has given to you, but I can change you into a form that will permit you to live always out upon the desert under the loving smiles of the star youth."

Her words filled the maiden with joy. She went with the witch woman upon the desert that night. There the old woman made a powerful drink from desert plants and told the maiden to drink it. As soon as she had done so her feet began to take root in the dry, sandy soil. Her arms turned to branches. Her black hair turned to leaves, and the maiden had become a new shrub which no Indian had seen in the desert before. As the wind blew the shrub seemed to murmur thanks to the witch woman.

When the sky youth saw what had happened, he leaned far out of an opening in his star lodge. He leaned so far out that the edges of the star broke with his weight, and he fell with sparkling pieces of star straight towards the maiden who had become a bush. The starry bits were shattered to fine dust that powdered the leaves of the bush with white. The youth was changed to purple blossoms. At last, the maiden and the sky youth were together.

The bush with white-dusted leaves and beautiful blossoms became known as the cenisa, or ash-covered bush. Today it is called the purple sage. Not many white people know the story of how it came to the desert.

The Man Who Became a Star

Inuit

There was once an old man who stood out on the ice waiting for the seal to come up to their breathing holes to breathe. But on the shore, just opposite where he was, a crowd of children were playing in a ravine, and time after time they frightened away a seal just as he was about to harpoon it.

At last, the old man grew angry with them for thus spoiling his catch, and cried out:

"Close up, Ravine, over those who are spoiling my hunting."

And at once the hillside closed over those children at play. One of them, who was carrying a little brother, had her fur coat torn. Then they all fell to screaming inside the hill, for they could not come out. And none could bring them food, only water that they were able to pour down a crack, and this they licked up from the sides.

At last, they all died of hunger.

And now the neighbors fell upon that old man who had shut up the children by magic in the hill. He took to flight, and the others ran after him.

But all at once he became bright, and rose up to heaven as a great star. We can see it now, in the west, when the lights begin to return after the great darkness. But it is low down, and never climbs high in the sky. And we call it Nâlaussartoq: he who stands and listens.

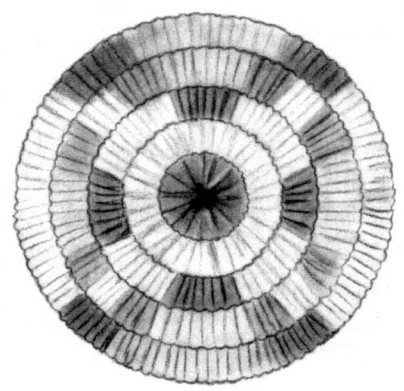

Tsul'kälû, the Slant-eyed Giant

Cherokee

A long time ago a widow lived with her one daughter at the old town of Känuga on Pigeon River. The girl was of age to marry, and her mother used to talk with her a good deal, and tell her she must be sure to take no one but a good hunter for a husband, so that they would have some one to take care of them and would always have plenty of meat in the house. The girl said such a man was hard to find, but her mother advised her not to be in a hurry, and to wait until the right one came.

Now the mother slept in the house while the girl slept outside in the âsï. One dark night a stranger came to the âsï wanting to court the girl, but she told him her mother would let her marry no one but a good hunter. "Well," said the stranger, "I am a great hunter," so she let him come in, and he stayed all night. Just before day he said he must go back now to his own place, but that he had brought some meat for her mother, and she would find it outside. Then he went away and the girl had not seen him. When day came, she went out and found there a deer, which she brought into the house to her mother, and told her it was a present from her new sweetheart. Her mother was pleased, and they had deer steaks for breakfast.

He came again the next night, but again went away before daylight, and this time he left two deer outside. The mother was more pleased this time, but said to her daughter, "I wish your sweetheart would bring us some wood." Now wherever he might be, the stranger knew their thoughts, so when he came the next time he said to the girl, "Tell your mother I have brought the wood"; and when she looked out in the morning there were several great trees lying in front of the door, roots and branches and all. The old woman was angry, and said, "He might have brought us some wood that we could use instead of whole trees that we can't split, to litter up the road with brush." The hunter knew what she said, and the next time he came he brought nothing, and when they looked out in the morning the trees were gone and there was no wood at all, so the old woman had to go after some herself.

Almost every night he came to see the girl, and each time he brought a deer or some other game, but still he always left before daylight. At last, her mother said to her, "Your husband always leaves before daylight. Why don't he wait? I want to see what kind of a son-in-law I have." When the girl told this to her husband, he said he could not let the old woman see him, because the sight would frighten her. "She wants to see you, anyhow," said the girl, and began to cry, until at last he had to consent, but warned her that her mother must not say that he looked frightful (*usga'së`ti'yu*).

The next morning, he did not leave so early, but stayed in the âsï, and when it was daylight, the girl went out and told her mother. The old woman came and looked in, and there she saw a great giant, with long slanting eyes (*tsul`kälû'*), lying doubled up on the floor, with his head against the rafters in the left-hand corner at the back, and his toes scraping the roof in the right-hand corner by the door. She gave only one look and ran back to the house, crying, *Usga'së`ti'yu! Usga'së`ti'yu!*

Tsul`kälû' was terribly angry. He untwisted himself and came out of the âsï, and said good-bye to the girl, telling her that he would never let her mother see him again, but would go back to his own country. Then he went off in the direction of Tsunegûñ'yï.

Soon after he left the girl had her monthly period. There was a very great flow of blood, and the mother threw it all into the river. One night after the girl had gone to bed in the âsï her husband came again to the door and said to her, "It seems you are alone," and asked where was the child. She said there had been none. Then he asked where was the blood, and she said that her mother had thrown it into the river. She told just where the place was, and he went there and found a small worm in the water. He took it up and carried it back to the âsï, and as he walked it took form and began to grow, until, when he reached the âsï, it was a baby girl that he was carrying. He gave it to his wife and said, "Your mother does not like me and abuses our child, so come and let us go to my home." The girl wanted to be with her husband, so, after telling her mother good-bye, she took up the child and they went off together to Tsunegûñ'yï.

Now, the girl had an older brother, who lived with his own wife in another settlement, and when he heard that his sister was married, he came to pay a visit to her and her new husband, but when he arrived at Känuga his mother told him his sister had taken her child and gone away with her husband, nobody knew where. He was sorry to see his mother so lonely, so he said he would go after his sister and try to find her and bring her back. It was easy to follow the footprints of the giant, and the young man went along the trail until he came to a place where they had rested, and there were tracks on the ground where a child had been lying and other marks as if a baby had been born there. He went on along the trail and came to another place where they had rested, and there were tracks of a baby crawling about and another lying on the ground. He went on and came to where they had rested again, and there were tracks of a child walking and another crawling about. He went on until he came where they had rested again, and there were tracks of one child running and another walking. Still, he followed the trail along the stream into the mountains, and came to the place where they had rested again, and this time there were footprints of two children running all about, and the footprints can still be seen in the rock at that place.

Twice again he found where they had rested. and then the trail led up the slope of Tsunegûñ'yï, and he heard the sound of a drum and voices, as if people were dancing inside the mountain. Soon he came to n eave like a doorway in the side of the mountain, but the rock was so steep and smooth that he could not climb tip to it, but could only just look over the edge and see the heads and shoulders of a great many people dancing inside. He saw his sister dancing among them and called to her to come out. She turned when she heard his voice, and as soon as the drumming stopped for a while, she came out to him, finding no trouble to climb down the rock, and leading her two little children by the hand. She was very glad to meet her brother and talked with him a long time, but did not ask him to come inside, and at last he went away without having seen her husband.

Several other times her brother came to the mountain, but always his sister met him outside, and he could never see her husband. After four years had passed, she came one day to her mother's house and said her husband had been hunting in the woods near by, and they were getting ready to start home to-morrow, and if her mother and brother would come early in the morning, they could see her husband. If they came too late for that, she said, they would find plenty of meat to take home. She went back into the woods, and the mother ran to tell her son. They came to the place early the next morning, but Tsul`kälû' and his family were already gone. On the drying poles they found the bodies of freshly killed deer hanging, as the girl had promised, and there were so many that they went back and told all their friends to come for them, and there were enough for the whole settlement.

Still the brother wanted to see his sister and her husband, so he went again to the mountain, and she came out to meet him. He asked to see her husband, and this time she told him to come inside with her. They went in as through a doorway, and inside he found it like a great townhouse. They seemed to be alone, but his sister called aloud, "He wants to see you," and from the air came a voice, "You can not see me until you put on a new dress, and then you can see me." "I am willing," said the young man, speaking to the unseen spirit, and from the air came the voice again, "Go back, then, and tell your people that to see me they must go into the townhouse and fast seven days, and in all that time they must not come out from the townhouse or raise the war whoop, and on the seventh day I shall come with new dresses for you to put on so that you can all see me."

The young man went back to Känuga and told the people. They all wanted to see Tsul`kälû', who owned all the game in the mountains, so they went into the townhouse and began the fast. They fasted the first day and the second and every day until the seventh-all but one man from another settlement, who slipped out every night when it was dark to get something to eat and slipped in again when no one was watching. On the morning of the seventh day the sun was just coming up in the east when they beard a great noise like the thunder of rocks rolling down the side of Tsunegûñ'yï. They were frightened and drew near together in the townhouse, and no one whispered.

Nearer and louder came the sound until it grew into an awful roar, and every one trembled and held his breath-all but one man, the stranger from the other settlement, who lost his senses from fear and ran out of the townhouse and shouted the war cry.

At once the roar stopped and for some time there was silence. Then they heard it again, but as if it were going farther away, and then farther and farther, until at last it died away in the direction of Tsunegûñ'yï, and then all was still again. The people came out from the townhouse, but there was silence, and they could see nothing but what had been seven days before.

Still the brother was not disheartened, but came again to see his sister, and she brought him into the mountain. He asked why Tsul`kälû' had not. brought the new dresses, as he had promised, and the voice from the air said, "I came with them, but you did not obey my word, but broke the fast and raised the war cry." The young man answered, "It was not done by our people, but by a stranger. If you will come again, we will surely do as you say." But the voice answered, "Now you can never see me." Then the young man could not say any more, and he went back to Känuga.

The Woman with the Iron Tail

Inuit

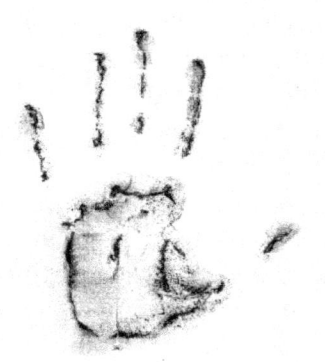

There was once a woman who had an iron tail. And more than this, she was also an eater of men. When a stranger came to visit her, she would wait until her guest had fallen asleep, and then she would jump up in the air, and fall down upon the sleeping one, who was thus pierced through by her tail.

Once there came a man to her house. And he lay down to sleep. And when she thought he had fallen asleep, she jumped up, and coming over the place where he lay, dropped down upon him. But the man was not asleep at all, and he moved aside so that she fell down on a stone and broke her tail.

The man fled out to his kayak. And she ran after.

When she reached him, she cried:

"Oh, if I could only thrust my knife into him."

And as she cried, the man nearly upset—for even her words had power.

"Oh, if only I could send my harpoon through her," cried the man in return. And so great was the power of his words that she fell down on the spot.

And then the man rowed away, and the woman never killed anyone after that, for her tail was broken.

The Evil Water Spirits

Tejas

Where did the big and ugly fishes and the snakes that swim in the water come from? The Indians know. From their forefathers comes this story.

A long time ago, before the Great Father had finished putting all the kinds of fish into the rivers and shady streams, there was an Indian woman who was blessed with twins. This Indian woman was a very proud mother, for her two little brown, black-eyed babies were good. to look at, and they had good tempers, and because of it, other women of the tribe also wished they might have twin babies.

It was in the spring time, and the little twins were about four years old when they began to tire of staying in their mother's wigwam. Their mother, one day, had gone with the other women of the tribe to pick wild berries that grow in the woods and around the brier patches. Some of these berries the Indians ate as soon as they picked them, but others they dried and stored to eat in winter, when a blanket of frost covered the field and woods and few birds and beasts could be found.

The mother had left the little children with their grandmother. This old woman was wrinkled and weak, and sleep comes easily to such people whose eyes are made heavy and tired with the weight of many years of hard work and troubles. Lying down on a deer skin inside the wigwam the grandmother began to watch the twins as they played near at hand just outside the door. The day was warm.

Even the locusts in the tree tops sang lazy, sleepy songs, and the breeze that moved the leafy limbs of the trees whispered softly. The old grandmother began to nod. Her head sank upon her arm. Without knowing it she fell asleep in the wigwam.

When the twins saw their grandmother was asleep, they put their heads together and whispered. Here was a fine chance to slip off and do something they had wanted to do for a long time. It was to do something that they had watched grown-up Indians do in the bayou that ran along the edge of the camp. The Indians waded in the bayou near its banks and bent down in the shallow water to dig up with their hands the tender roots of the plants called "Yonkupins" whose broad green leaves lift well above the surface of the bayou. These roots were good to eat. The little twins had seen the Indians gathering them and they wanted to gather them too.

Now their mother was away and their grandmother was asleep and they had a chance to do it. Without a word they slipped away from the wigwam when nobody was looking, and they ran without making a noise with their little buck-skin moccasins along a grassy path that led towards the bayou.

And now they were standing on the brink of a shallow place where a tongue of the bayou ran back into a low place in the banks. Everything was still among the high reeds that grew on the banks and leaned over the water. The twins looked down. They could see the bottom and weeds growing on it. What was in the weeds? They had been told by their mother that evil spirits were there, for she wanted to frighten them so they would not want to go near the bayou and be drowned. But they saw nothing, and they waded in, hand in hand.

They saw the broad green pads or leaves of lily plants floating a little way from the bank, and they knew that the roots were underneath, growing in the soft mud. Carefully they waded towards them. The water rose up to their knees. They were not afraid because they had not found the evil spirits their mother had told them about. They waded farther. The water was up to their waists. Now they were among the lily pads, and the long stems of the plants slipped against their brown bodies and tickled them. Here was the place to feel around in the bottom for the roots. The little boy and girl bent over and stretched their short arms down into the water around their feet. They had to bend until their chins were in the water and all their bodies but their heads were beneath the surface, but still they were not afraid, because even yet they had not seen the evil spirits their mother told were there. It was so nice to be feeling with their fingers in the cool mud. The weeds growing on the bottom tickled their toes, and the leaves of the lily plants rubbed against their faces.

But just then, when everything seemed so easy and beautiful something happened. In pulling at a root one of the twins suddenly slipped and fell. Her head went under water. Then she became frightened, and with a scared cry she caught at her brother and pulled him down too. The evil spirits seemed to have them now. The lily stems wound around their bodies as they struggled.

The warm water filled their open mouths as they tried to call their mother. They tried to get out of the clinging lily stems but they only slipped into deeper water and became wrapped tighter with the stems that were like ropes. They could not call for help for their mouths were filling with water. They could not get back to the bank for their heads were under water and they could not reach the bottom any more. The bright sun faded out swiftly, the songs of the birds were heard no more, the muddy water blinded their eyes and everything became dark. Poor little Indian twins! The evil water spirits they could not see had trapped them.

After a while the Indians came and found the children lying in each other's arms in the shallow water. They could not hear their poor mother wailing, nor could they hear their old grandmother moaning, and swinging to and fro in her sorrow. They could not see their father as he stood tall and still looking down at them on the bank while he sternly kept the grief of a father's heart from showing in a warrior's face.

That night, while the mother was sitting beside her twins for the last time, watching over their bodies before they were buried with their toys in the earth, she asked the Great Spirit to grant her a wish. For the sake of the other babies of the tribe she asked that the evil spirits of the water be given shapes that could be seen, so that the other babies would see them iii the water and be frightened away from them.

The Great Spirit granted the wish of this unselfish mother. He gave to those evil spirits the shapes that all men fear, the shapes of the alligator, the big snapping turtle, the gar fish with his rows of wicked teeth, and the snake known as the water moccasin. From that time the little Indian boys and girls could see those evil spirits and keep away from them.

The Great Leech of Tlanusi'yï

Cherokee

The spot where Valley River joins Hiwassee, at Murphy, in North Carolina, is known among the Cherokees as Tlanusi'yï, "The Leech place," and this is the story they tell of it:

Just above the junction is a deep hole in Valley River, and above it is a ledge of rock running across the stream, over which people used to go as on a bridge. On the south side the trail ascended a high bank, from which they could look down into the water. One day some men going along the trail saw a great red object, full as large as a house, lying on the rock ledge in the middle of the stream below them.

As they stood wondering what it could be they saw it unroll--and then they knew it was alive--and stretch itself out along the rock until it looked like a great leech with red and white stripes along its body. It rolled up into a ball and again stretched out at full length, and at last crawled down the rock and was out of sight in the deep water. The water began to boil and foam, and a great column of white spray was thrown high in the air and came down like a waterspout upon the very spot where the men had been standing, and would have swept them all into the water but that they saw it in time and ran from the place.

More than one person was carried down in this way, and their friends would find the body afterwards lying upon the bank with the ears and nose eaten off, until at last the people were afraid to go across the ledge any more, on account of the great leech, or even to go along that part of the trail. But there was one young fellow who laughed at the whole story, and said that he was not afraid of anything in Valley River, as he would show them. So, one day he painted his face and put on his finest buckskin and started off toward the river, while all the people followed at a distance to see what might happen. Down the trail he went and out upon the ledge of rock, singing in high spirits:

> Tlanu'si gäe'ga digi'gäge
> Dakwa'nitlaste'stï.
> I'll tie red leech skins
> On my legs for garters.

But before he was half way across the water began to boil into white foam and a great wave rose and swept over the rock and carried him down, and he was never seen again.

Just before the Removal, sixty years ago, two women went out upon the ledge to fish. Their friends warned them of the danger, but one woman who had her baby on her back said, "There are fish there and I'm going to have some; I'm tired of this fat meat." She laid the child down on the rock and was preparing the line when the water suddenly rose and swept over the ledge, and would have carried off the child but that the mother ran in time to save it.

The great leech is still there in the deep hole, because when people look down, they see something alive moving about on the bottom, and although they can not distinguish its shape on account of the ripples on the water, yet they know it is the leech. Some say there is an underground waterway across to Nottely River, not far above the mouth, where the

127

river bends over toward Murphy, and sometimes the leech goes over there and makes the water boil as it used to at the rock ledge. They call this spot on Nottely "The Leech place" also.

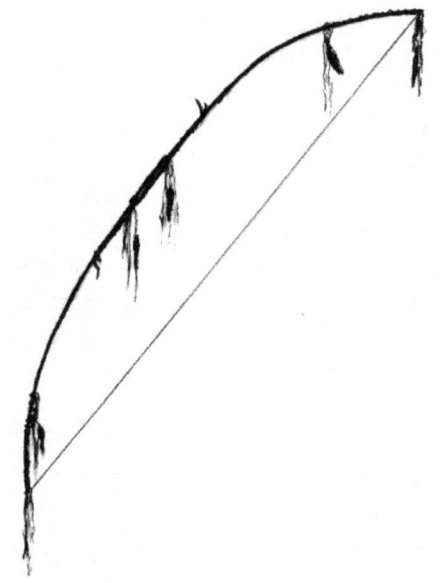

A Man Chased by the Ancient of Lizards

Seneca

Once there was a large village where people lived happily and had plenty of meat. At the end of the village lived a man whom few persons noticed.

One night that man had a dream. His dream said, "Something is going to happen to the people of this village. You must tell them to move away within ten days."

The next morning the man went to the center of the village, gathered the people and told his dream. Some believed in the dream others did not. Five days later those who had believed joined those who had not, and paid no heed to the dream.

The fifth night the man dreamed again and his dream said, "We know that the people do not heed your warning. But save yourself. Three days from now take all your arrows and climb the hill on the east side of the village till you come to a large rock. The rock is hollow. Go inside of it and you will find a hole in the ground. Look through the hole and you will see all that is going on in the village.

"The people will be destroyed by Big Head. Five days from now, at midday, there will be a terrible outcry. When the cry dies away, you must begin to shoot through the hole, for as soon as the people are destroyed the monster will track you. You will save your life if you shoot all your arrows at it before it reaches the hole.

"When the monster is dead, take from the back of its head a piece of skin together with the hair, which is very long. The skin will be of use to you, for it has great power. Wind the hair around your body next to your skin and declare that there is nothing that you cannot do.

"At night, when it is dark enough not to be seen, go North a short distance and you will find a tree turned up by the roots. You must not be frightened. I shall give you something which will be of great use to you."

After this dream the man was gloomy and unhappy. When the time came, he took his bundle of arrows and left the village. He didn't take his wife or children for they did not believe in the dream. Just at sunset he came to a large rock on the side of the hill. He found the opening and going into it crept along till he thought he was under the center of the rock. There he found a space high enough for him to stand in. He lay down and slept.

The next morning a deer was standing near the opening. He killed it, roasted some of the meat and ate it.

The fifth day, as the man sat on the rock, he heard a great noise coming from the South. As the sound approached the village, he saw something that looked like smoke, saw that trees were falling, and falling toward the village.

When the noise reached the village, the man took his position opposite the opening in the ground. It seemed to him that the village was right at hand. He heard the screaming of the people and saw the cabins torn to pieces and hurled into the air.

Big Head missed one man, and when all the others were destroyed, he laughed, and said, "This world is not large enough for him to hide in."

When the man saw that trees were falling toward the East, he knew that Big Head had found his trail, and he strung his bow and began to shoot through the hole as rapidly as possible. When only two arrows were left, he saw a great black Head not far away. He shot his last arrow; the roar ceased, the Head fell and he heard it say, "You have killed me!"

The man went to where the Head lay and found in it every arrow he had shot. "I must do as my dream said," thought he, so he took a part of the scalp, tied it around his body and said, "You must always help me. You must not let me be overpowered by anyone."

He climbed to the top of the hill quickly, for now he could go very fast. He found a good place and built a brush hut. "I must have plenty of meat," thought he, and going out he saw deer, bears and all kinds of game. He killed what he wanted. To skin the deer and bears he had merely to take hold of the skin of the head and pull; with no effort the skin came from the whole carcass. He made a brush shed and hung the meat up to dry.

When it began to grow dark, the man started toward the North, as his dream had told him to do. He had not gone far when he came to a fallen tree, the roots turned out of the ground. When half way around the tree, he saw Meteor with his great mouth open.

When Meteor saw that the man wasn't frightened, he laughed and said, "Take one of my teeth, it will be of great use to you. It will enable you to change yourself into any form you like."

The man took a double tooth, the one farthest back in Meteor's jaw.

Then Meteor said, "You will live always and you will have great power, but you and I must always counsel with each other. Now we will part."

Meteor flew off through the air and the man went back to his hut. He made up his mind that the hut would be his home. He stayed there a long time then getting lonesome, he said to himself, "I will go and see if I can find people anywhere."

He turned into a hawk and flew toward the southwest. As he rose high in the air he looked down on the ground. After a while he saw, in the West, something that made him think people were living there. Then he began to come down. He came lower and lower and when near the ground saw a village. He said to himself, "I will eat up the people who live in that village."

He turned into a great bear and, beginning at the first house, ate up every person he could find. When he thought he had eaten everybody, he saw, off at the edge of the village, a little hut with smoke rising from it. In the hut he found a man and woman and several children. He ate them all.

"I have finished," said he, and changed himself to a man.

He stood around a while, then, seeing a trail he followed it, but had not gone far when he met a woman who was very handsome.

"Where do you live?" asked he.

"Over there in the cabin at the edge of the village."

"You had better go home with me for there is no one living in that cabin. All the people are dead."

"I must see first," said the woman.

They went back to the village and to the hut where he had found the man, woman, and children. She was the eldest child of the family. Seeing blood on the ground she began to cry. The man put his hand on the top of her head. That minute she was senseless. He shook her and as he shook, she became a gnat. He changed himself to a hawk and putting the gnat under his wing flew up and off in the direction of his hut. He got there quickly, then he changed to a man and shook the gnat back to her natural form and size.

"This is your home," said he, "You must take care of the meat and the house."

One night while the two were sitting in the hut, the man heard a noise outside as though someone were coming on a run. The door was pushed open and a man came in, and said, "I have come to warn you. You have made yourself into two. NYAGWAIHE (the Ancient of Bears) --is jealous of you and has said, 'There is a man over there who is very powerful, but I will overpower him and eat him.'"

"To-morrow the Bear will come. You must go East till you reach a high stony hill. When the Bear tries to attack you, jump from one rock to another. It will spring after you. When it falls, you may feel safe. This is what I had to tell you. Now I will go."

The next morning the woman saw that her husband was gloomy and sad.

"What is the matter?" asked she.

"I am thinking of what will happen to me at midday."

The woman had neither seen nor heard the man who spoke to her husband though she was right there in the hut. He and the man who came to him were so powerful in spirit that they alone heard and saw each other.

When it was nearly midday, the man started for the rocks, leaving his wife. He seated himself on the highest rock and waited. Just at midday he heard a great noise, then another nearer; the third was right at the rock.

There was a whoop and a voice said, "I am the strongest of the strong. Nothing can overpower me."

It was NYAGWAIHE (the Ancient of Bears). The Bear leaped on to the rock where the man stood. The man sprang to the next rock, the Bear close behind him. In this way they sprang from one rock to another till the man was tired. As he looked ahead, the next rock looked farther off than the others had been. He made a great effort and just reached it. The Bear was right behind him. It sprang, but falling short, hit its jaws on the edge of the rock and went down.

The man jumped to the ground. As he struck the ground he looked back and saw the rock he had just left turn over on to the Bear.

"That is what I said," thought the man. "There is nothing that can overpower me."

He went back to his hut. He was very happy.

One day when the man and woman were sitting by the fire, they heard somebody approaching the hut. The man opened the door and saw the friend who had twice warned him of danger. The woman saw him too.

The man said, "Your life is in danger but I will try and save you. Rub your wife's head with your hands, she will turn to *oshada* (*oshada* is like the dusty vapor flying on a road in dry weather). Tell her to follow you wherever you go, but she must leave the hut before you do, you will stay here as long as you can, then run directly South. I am going now, but I will come to you again."

In the morning the man rubbed the woman's head and said, "Let my wife become a dusty vapor."

While he rubbed, she became a vapor on his hand. With his other hand he brushed the vapor off in the direction it was to go. Then he piled up his meat and said in a loud voice, "I give this meat to you flesh-eating animals that live in the woods."

He went southward from the hut to an elm tree that was smooth up to where it branched off. He climbed the tree and sat in the crotch. Soon he began to feel weak, and he thought, "There must be something near." He looked everywhere but saw no one.

Taking out the Meteor tooth he dampened it with saliva, rubbed his finger over it, then rubbed his eyes, and said, "Now I can see everything that is going on, even down in the ground."

He looked into the earth and saw, deep down, a tree and on the tree was a monster Lizard. He watched it as it climbed slowly up the tree. When it was near the top, the man grew very faint.

The Lizard was the largest of the ancient blue Lizards (DZAINOS GOWA). It came out of the ground in the heart of the tree that the man was sitting on. The man leaped to another tree.

That instant the Lizard was where the man had been sitting and it called out, "You are smart but I shall overpower you."

It sprang toward the man; the man leaped to another tree and then from tree to tree, the Lizard following.

At the edge of a hill was a great rock. The man ran to the rock and from the rock leaped into the air and came down on a mountain far away. He ran directly south along the ridge of the mountain, then went down on the opposite side to a wide valley. He ran across the valley and had begun to climb a second mountain when he heard the Lizard coming down the mountain he had just descended on the other side of the valley. It was dark now but the man continued to run, ran all night.

In the morning he saw an opening on the other side of which was a low hill, and smoke of some kind. He reached the foot of the hill and turning saw the Lizard had just come to the opening. It raised its paw and struck the man's footprint on the trail. That instant the man fell to the ground. As he fell his friend was there and said, "Get up! You will die if you fall in this way."

He lifted him and pushed him into a run, urging him to hurry. The man felt stronger and again ran fast from valley to valley, the Lizard always about the same distance behind.

All at once the man fell again. Right away his friend was there. He lifted him to his feet saying, "Keep up courage," and pushed him into a run. Again, he felt stronger and ran faster.

It was a very dark night; he ran against a great maple tree. As he hit the tree he went straight through. This happened many times in the night. Whenever the man hit a tree, he went through it.

For eight days and nights the Lizard chased the man. When it found out that he went through trees it threw its power ahead and made the trees so hard that the man could no longer go through them.

The ninth night the Lizard commanded a terrible rain storm to come and the night to be so dark that the man couldn't see where he was going. The man ran till midnight without once hitting a tree. Just at midnight he hit one and was thrown far back.

That moment his friend was there, and said, "Do all you can," and taking hold of his hand he led him and they went faster than the man had gone alone.

The two ran together till daylight, then the friend left and the man went on alone. He began to be very weak. The

Lizard was coming nearer and its strokes on the tracks were more frequent; the man fell oftener.

Night came and the Lizard made it terribly dark. The man ran against a tree and bounded far back. The Lizard was so near that the man fell behind him. The Lizard struck the tree and was thrown back also. The man was up and running forward again. The Lizard was just upon him and was reaching out to seize him when the man fell, as it seemed to him, into a hole in the ground. He thought,

"Well, I am near my end; when I strike, I shall be dashed to pieces."

He kept falling and as he fell, he got sleepy. Looking up he saw the Lizard coming down on the side of the hole, winding around and around. The man fell asleep. After a time, he woke up and was still falling and the Lizard was still pursuing him.

At last, the man landed on his feet. He seemed to have come out of the hole. He looked around and saw a beautiful country. "My friend told me to go toward the South," thought he, and he ran on in that direction.

As the man ran, he knew that the Lizard was behind him coming very fast. "Now I shall die," thought he. He closed his eyes and kept on, thinking, "I will not see when it reaches me."

He ran a long time, then opened his eyes and looked around. He didn't see the Lizard but he kept running. Soon he came to a house and going in found an old man.

The old man looked up and said, "My grandson, I am glad you have come. I have been waiting for you. You are bringing with you, what I have wanted to eat. Stand back there, Lizard and I will fight alone. We will see if he is as powerful as he thinks he is."

The Lizard came to the house and asked, "Where is the man I have been chasing?"

"Here I am," answered the old man.

"You are not the man."

"I am, but if you think there is another man here, you will not hunt for him till you overpower me."

"Come outside," said the Lizard, "there isn't room in here."

"Very well," said the old man and getting up he went outside. They began to fight. The Lizard tore the old man's flesh. It came together again and healed. The old man tore off Lizard's forelegs, but Lizard didn't give up; the two fought till Lizard was torn to pieces.

When the old man convinced himself that the pieces were not alive, he hung them up in the house and called to his grandson, "Come out! I have killed the Lizard that you were afraid of. I have been wishing for this kind of meat for a long time."

The old man boiled some of the meat in a large kettle. In a small kettle he cooked bear meat for his grandson.

While the meat was cooking, he put corn in a pounder and with a few strokes it was flour. Then he made bread and began eating.

When he had eaten every bit of the great Lizard, he said, "I thank you, my grandson, this meat will last me for many years. You must stay here till you are rested and cured, for you have been poisoned by the power of the Lizard."

The old man was the oldest of the Flying Meteors. One day he said to the man, "I want you to see what I have planted."

They went a short distance from the cabin to a field where something was growing.

"This is ones (corn)," said the old man.

There were tall stalks with ears on them as long as the man was tall and the kernels were as large as a man's head.

The old man said, "Let us go to the other side of the field."

There the man saw a field where different kinds of corn were growing.

They went to a third field where something was growing and the old man said, "These are squashes." They were very large.

They passed the squash field and went back to the cabin.

The next day the man said good-bye to his grandfather and started for home. He traveled till he came to a village. He went to the chief's house and a woman who was there looked at him, then asked, "Have you ever heard of a man who sent his wife away in the form of vapor?"

He thought a little while, then remembered, and answered, "I have. I did that myself."

"I am your wife," said the woman.

The man had had so much trouble that he had forgotten about his wife, but he was glad to find her. They went home together and lived happily.

The Origin of Death

Cochiti

They were coming up from Shipap. One of their children became sick and they did not know what was the trouble with him. They had never seen sickness before. They said to the Shkoyo (curing society) chief, "Perhaps our Mother in Shipap will help us. Go back and ask her to take away this trouble." He went back to our Mother and she said to him, "The child is dead. If your people did not die, the world would fill up and there would be no place for you to live. When you die, you will come back to Shipap to five with me. Keep on traveling and do not be troubled when your people die."

He returned to his people and told them what our Mother had said. In those days they treated one another as brothers, all the Indians of all the pueblos. They planted corn with the digging stick and they were never tired; they dug trenches to irrigate their fields. The corn ripened in one day. When they came to Frijoles they separated, and the different pueblos went their own ways.

The Giant Cloud-Swallower

A Tale of Cañon De Chelly

Deep down in cañons of the Southwest, especially where they are joined by other cañons, the traveler may see standing forth from or hugging the angles of the cliffs, great towering needles of stone--weird, rugged, fantastic, oftentimes single, as often--like gigantic wind-stripped trees with lesser trees standing beside them--double or treble. Seen suddenly at a turn in the cañon these giant stones startle the gazer with their monstrous and human proportions, like giants, indeed, at bay against the sheer rock walls, protecting their young, who appear anon to crouch at the knees of their fathers or cling to their sides.

Few white men behold these statuesque stones in the moonlight, or in the gray light and white mists of the morning. At midday they seem dead or asleep while standing; but when the moon is shining above them and the wanderer below looks up to them, lo! the moon stands still and these mighty crags start forth, advancing noiselessly. His back is frozen, and even in the yielding sand his feet are held fast by terror--a delicious, ghostly terror, withal! Still, he gazes fascinated, and as the shadow of the moonlight falls toward him over the topmost crest, lo, again! its crown is illumined and circled as if by a halo of snow-light, and back and forth from this luminous fillet over that high stony brow, black hair seems to tumble and gather.

Again, beheld in the dawn-light, when the mists are rising slowly and are waving to and fro around the giddy columns, hiding the cliffs behind them, these vast pinnacles seem to nod and to waver or to sway themselves backward and forward, all as silently as before. Soon, when the sun is risen and the mists from below fade away, the wind blows more mist from the mesa; you see clouds of it pour from the cliff edge, just behind and above these great towers, and shimmer against the bright sky; but as soon as these clouds pass the crag-nests they are lost in the sunlight around them-lost so fast, as yet others come on, that the stone giants seem to drink them.

Of such rocks, according to their variety and local surroundings, the Zuñis relate many tales which are so ingenious and befitting that if we believed, as the Zuñis do, that in the time of creation when all things were young and soft and were therefore easily fashioned by whatever chanced to befall them--into this thing or that thing, into this plant or that plant, this animal or that, and so on endlessly through a dramatic story longer than Shakespeare or the Bible--we would fain believe also as he does in the quaint incidents of these stories of the time when all things were new and the world was becoming as we see it now.

One of these tales, a variant of others pertaining to particular standing rocks in the west, south, or east, is told of that wonder to all beholders, "El Capitan," of the Canon de Chelly in the north. No one who has seen this stupendous rock column can fail to be interested in the following legend, or will fail to realize how, as this introduction endeavors to make plainer, the Zuñi poet and philosopher of olden times built up a story which he verily believed quite sufficient to account for the great shaft of sandstone and its many details and surroundings. --F. H. C.

Häki Suto, or Foretop Knot, he whose hair was done up over his forehead like a quail's crest, lived among the great cliffs of the north long ago, when the world was new. He was a giant, so tall that men called him *Lo Ikwithltchunona*, or the Cloud-swallower. A devourer of men was he, --men were his meat--yea, and a drinker of their very substance was he, for the cloud-breaths of the beloved gods, and souls of the dead, whence descend rains, even these were his drink. Wherefore the People of the Cliffs sought to slay him, and hero after hero perished thuswise. Wherefore, too, snow ceased in the north and the west; rain ceased in the south and the east; the mists of the mountains above were drunk up; the waters of the valleys below were dried up; corn withered in the fields; men hungered and died in the cliffs.

Then came the Twin Gods of War, Áhaiyúta and Mátsailéma, who in play staked the lives of foes and fierce creatures. "Lo! it is not well with our children, men," said they. "Let us destroy this Häki Suto, the swallower of clouds," said they.

They were walking along the trail which leads southward to the Smooth-rocks-descending.

"O, grandchildren, where be ye wending?" said a little, little quavering voice. They looked, --the younger, then the elder. There on the tip of a grass-stalk, waving her banner of down-stuff, stood their grandmother, Spinner of Meshes.

"The Spider! Our Grandmother Spider!" cried one of the gods to the other. "Ho! grandmother, was that you calling?" shouted they to her.

"Yea, children; where wend ye this noon-day?

"A-warring we are going," said they. "Look now!"

> "No beads for to broider your awning
> Have fallen this many a morning."

"Aha, wait ye! Whom ye seek, verily I know him well," said the Spider-woman.

> "Like a tree fallen down from the mountain
> He lies by the side of the cliff-trail
> And feigns to sleep there, yet is wary.
> I will sew up his eyes with my down-cords.
> Then come ye and smite him,
> grandchildren."

She ran ahead. There lay Häki Suto, his legs over the trail where men journeyed. Great, like the trunks and branches of pine trees cast down by a wind-storm, were his legs arching over the pathway, and when some one chanced to come by, the giant would call out: "Good morning!" and bid him "pass right along under." "I am old and rheumatic," he would continue, oh, so politely! "Do not mind my rudeness, therefore; run right along under; never fear, run right along under!" But when the hunter tried to pass, *kúutsu!* Häki Suto would snatch him up and cast him over the cliff to be eaten by the young Forehead-cresters.

The Spider stepped never so lightly, and climbed up behind his great ear, and then busily wove at her web, to and fro, up and down, and in and out of his eyelashes she busily plied at her web.

"Pesk the birds and buzz creatures!" growled the giant, twitching this way and that his eyebrows. which tickled;

146

but he would not stir, --for he heard the War-gods coming, and thought them fat hunters and needs must feign sleepy.

"And these? Ha! ha! They begin to sing, as was their fearless wont sometimes. Häki Suto never looked, but yawned and drawled as they came near, and nearer. "Never mind, my children, pass right along under, pass right along under; I am lame and tired this morning," said he.

Áhaiyúta ran to the left. Mátsailéma ran to the right. Häki Suto sprang up to catch them, but his eyes were so blinded with cobwebs that he missed them and feigned to fall, crying: "Ouch! my poor back! my poor back! Pass right along under, my children, it was only a crick in my back. Ouch! Oh, my poor back!" But they whacked him over the head and stomach till he stiffened and died. Then shouting "*So ho!*" they shoved him over the Cliff.

The Navahos say that the grandmother tied him there by the hair--by his topknot--where you see the white streaks on the pillar, so they say; but it's the birds that streak the pillar, and this is the way. When Häki Suto fell, his feet drove far into the sands, and the Storm-gods rushed in to the aid of their children, the War-gods, and drifted his blood-bedrenched carcass all over with sand, whence he dried and hardened to stone. When the young ones saw him falling, they forthwith flocked up to devour him, making loud clamor. But the Twain, seeing this, made after them too and twisted the necks of all save only the tallest (who was caught in the sands with his father) and flung them aloft to the winds, whereby one became instantly the Owl, who twists her head wholly around whensoever she pleases, and stares as though frightened and strangled; and another the Falcon became, who perches and nests to this day on the crest of his sand-covered father, the Giant

Cloud-drinker. And the Falcons cry ever and ever "'Tis father; O father!" ("*Tí-tätchu ya-tätchu.*")

But, fearing that never again would the waters refreshen their cañons, our ancients who dwelt in the cliffs fled away to the southward and eastward--all save those who had perished aforetime; they are dead in their homes in the cliff-towns, dried, like their cornstalks that died when the rain stopped long, long ago, when all things were new.

Thus shortens my story.

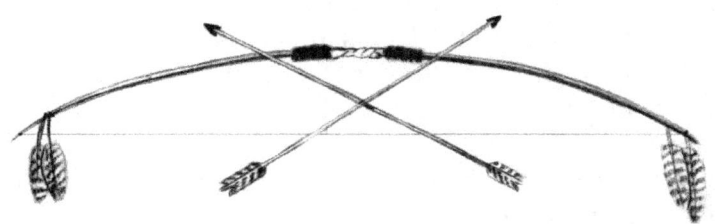

Kumagdlak and the Living Arrows

Inuit

Kumagdlak, men say, lived apart from his fellows. He had a wife, and she was the only living being in the place beside himself.

One day his wife was out looking for stones to build a fireplace, and looking out over the sea, she saw many enemies approaching.

"An umiak and kayaks," she cried to her husband. And he was ill at ease on hearing this, for he lay in the house with a bad leg.

"My arrows—bring my arrows!" he cried. And his wife saw that all his arrows lay there trembling. And that was because their points were made of the shinbones of men. And they trembled because their master was ill at ease.

Kumagdlak had made himself arrows, and feathered them with birds' feathers. He was a great wizard, and by breathing with his own breath upon those arrows he could give them life, and cause them to fly towards his enemies

149

and kill them. And when he himself stood unprotected before the weapons of his enemies, he would grasp the thong of the pouch in which his mother had carried him as a child, and strike out with it, and then all arrows aimed at him would fly wide of their mark.

Now all the enemies hauled up on shore, and the eldest among them cried out:

"Kumagdlak! It is time for you to go out and taste the water in the land of the dead under the earth—or perhaps you will go up into the sky?"

"That fate is more likely to be yours," answered Kumagdlak.

And standing at the entrance to his tent, he aimed at them with his bow. If but the first arrow could be sent whirling over the boats, then he knew that none of them would be able to harm him. He shot his arrow, and it flew over the boats. Then he aimed at the old man who had spoken, and that arrow cut through the string of the old man's bow, and pierced the old man himself. Then he began shooting down the others, his wife handing him the arrows as he shot. The men from the boats shot at him, but all their arrows flew wide. And his enemies grew fewer and fewer, and at last they fled. And now Kumagdlak took all the bodies down by the shore and plundered them, taking their knives, and when the boats had got well out to sea, he called up a great storm, so that all the others perished.

But the waves washed the bodies this way and that along the coast, until the clothes were worn off them.

Here ends this story.

The Stick That Sang

Yaqui

On the Rio Yaqui lived two brothers. They lived with their mother and father. One day they went to some hill, I don't know just where, to pan gold. There were two canyons at this place; one came from the north, and the other from the east. The canyons met there. When it rained, the water brought down gold. The boys went there to find gold. The smaller boy rode a burro and the older one, a mule.

Miguel, the older boy, said, "José, you go up that canyon. I saw a lot of gold up there."

Jose took his burro and went. Miguel stayed where he was. There was gold there, but in little grains, only as big as wheat.

José hunted up in the canyon for a long time. At last, he found a big nugget, a ball of gold. When Miguel came up, he said, "Miguel, I have found a big nugget."

"Let me see it."

"I don't want to show it to you."

"I want to see it," said Miguel.

The two boys fought, and Miguel hit José on the head with a rock and killed him.

Miguel took the ball of gold. He buried José and piled up rocks on the grave. He let José's burro go, and then left.

When he arrived at his home his father said, "Where is José?"

"I lost him," said Miguel.

"Where?" asked the father.

"Over there."

"Well," said the father, "let's go hunt for him."

They set off and encountered the little burro on the road. "Who knows what happened," said the father slowly. He began to cry. Miguel took him to another hill. They found no one.

Many months passed and the muleteers who always went along the road didn't know anything about it. After six months, a straight little stick grew up out of the head of the dead boy. There was a little button on top of the stick.

A muleteer stopped there one day at noon to let his animal's graze. He saw the little stick. "How strange," he said, and he grasped it with his hand. Then the stick began to sing, saying, "For a ball of gold, my brother killed me."

The muleteer cut the stick off and carried it with him very carefully.

After traveling three days, he arrived at a pueblo called San Marcial. He took the little stick about the streets shouting, "I carry a stick that sings. Two *reales* to hear it."

"What is this?" said the people. "He carries a stick that knows how to sing? It couldn't be anything. It's not going to sing. Let's see. Let's hear it sing."

The muleteer walked about, holding out his hat. The people threw in money. His hat was almost filled.

Then the muleteer grasped the stick and it sang thus, "For a ball of gold, a ball of gold, my brother killed me."

The people were frightened. "What can this be? His brother killed him for a ball of gold?" Many heard.

Now the muleteer went to another pueblo. He went through the streets calling again, "I carry a little stick that sings all by itself!" Many people gathered. They threw money into his hat. Then he made the stick sing. It always sang, "For a ball of gold, my brother killed me."

Then the muleteer went on to the pueblo of Vicam. Here there were no streets, only one house here, another there, just rancherías. Now the father of Jose was living there and the muleteer said to him, "Wouldn't you like to hear a little stick sing""

"Yes," said the old man.

"I will make it sing," said the muleteer. He grasped the stick and it sang, "For a ball of gold, my brother killed me."

"That sounds like my own son!" said the old man. "It sounds like José, the son I lost in the mountains."

Everything was discovered against Miguel. But Miguel said that he did not kill his brother. The father did not know what to believe.

People came from the eight pueblos. And each pueblo had to say one word. Each man who had a thought spoke. And one of them said, "Whoever killed José would be carrying a ball of gold."

And it was found that Miguel was carrying a ball of gold. For that reason, he was discovered.

He was stood up in front of six soldiers. They shot him in the chest and he died. They buried him. There it ends.

The Tsundige'wï

Cherokee

Once some young men of the Cherokee set out to see what was in the world and traveled south until they came to a tribe of little people called *Tsundige'wï*, with very queer shaped bodies, hardly tall enough to reach up to a man's knee, who had no houses, but lived in nests scooped in the sand and covered over with dried grass. The little fellows were so weak and puny that they could not fight at all, and were in constant terror from the wild geese and other birds that used to come in great flocks from the south to make war upon them.

Just at the time that the travelers got there they found the little men in great fear, because there was a strong wind blowing from the south and it blew white feathers and down along the sand, so that the Tsundige'wï knew their enemies were coming not far behind. The Cherokee asked them why, they did not defend themselves, but they said they could not, because they did not know how. There was no time to make bows and arrows, but the travelers told them to take sticks for clubs, and showed them where to strike the birds on the necks to kill them.

The wind blew for several days, and at last the birds came, so many that they were like a great cloud in the air, and alighted on the sands. The little men ran to their nests, and the birds followed and stuck in their long bills to pull them out and eat them. This time. though, the Tsundige'wï had their clubs, and they struck the birds on the neck, as the

Cherokee had shown them, and killed so many that at last the others were glad to spread their wings and fly away again to the south.

The little men thanked the Cherokee for their help and gave them the best they had until the travelers went on to see the other tribes. They heard afterwards that the birds came again several times, but that the Tsundige'wï always drove them off with their clubs, until a flock of sandhill cranes came. They were so tall that the little men could not reach up to strike them on the neck, and so at last the cranes killed them all.

The Ice Man

Cherokee

Once when the people were burning the woods in the fall the blaze set fire to a poplar tree, which continued to burn until the fire went down into the roots and burned a great hole in the ground. It burned and burned, and the hole grew constantly larger, until the people became frightened and were afraid it would burn the whole world. They tried to put out the fire, but it had gone too deep, and they did not know what to do.

At last, some one said there was a man living in a house of ice far in the north who could put out the fire, so messengers were sent, and after traveling a long distance they came to the ice house and found the Ice Man at home. He was a little fellow with long hair hanging down to the ground in two plaits. The messengers told him their errand and he at once said, "O yes, I can help you," and began to unplait his hair.

When it was all unbraided, he took it up in one band and struck it once across his other hand, and the messengers felt a wind blow against their cheeks. A second time he struck his hair across his hand, and a light rain began to fall. The third time he struck his hair across his open hand there was sleet mixed with the raindrops, and when he struck the fourth time great hailstones fell upon the ground, as if they had come out from the ends of his hair. "Go back now," said the Ice Man, "and I shall be there to-morrow." So, the messengers returned to their people, whom they found still gathered helplessly about the great burning pit.

The next-day while they were all watching about the fire there came a wind from the north, and they were afraid, for they knew that it came from the Ice Man. But the wind only made the fire blaze up higher. Then a light rain began to fall, but the drops seemed only to make the fire hotter. Then the shower turned to a heavy rain, with sleet and hail that killed the blaze and made clouds of smoke and steam rise from the red coals.

The people fled to their homes for shelter, and the storm rose to a whirlwind that drove the rain into every burning crevice and piled great hailstones over the embers, until the fire was dead and even the smoke ceased. When at last it was all over and the people returned, they found a lake where the burning pit had been, and from below the water came a sound as of embers still crackling.

The Thunder Spirits

Inuit

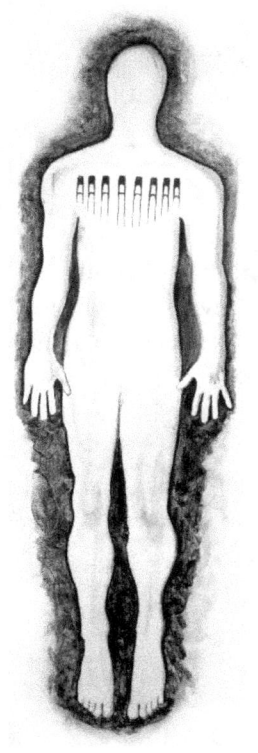

Two sisters, men say, were playing together, and their father could not bear to hear the noise they made, for he had but few children, and was thus not want to hear any kind of noise. At last, he began to scold them, and told them to go farther away with their playing.

When the girls grew up, and began to understand things, they desired to run away on account of their father's scolding. And at last, they set out, taking with them only a little dogskin, and a piece of boot skin, and a fire stone. They went up into a high mountain to build themselves a house there.

Their father and mother made search for them in vain, for the girls kept hiding themselves; they had grown to be true mountain dwellers, keeping far from the places of men. Only the reindeer hunters saw them now and again, but the girls always refused to go back to their kin.

And when at last the time came when they must die of hunger, they turned into evil spirits, and became thunder.

When they shake their dried boot skin, then the gales come up, the south-westerly gales. And great fire is seen in the heavens whenever they strike their fire stone, and the rain pours down whenever they shed tears.

Their father held many spirit callings, hoping to make them return. But this he ceased to do when he found that they were dead.

But men say that after those girls had become spirits, they returned to the places of men, frightening many to death. They came first of all to their father and mother, because of the trouble they had made. The only one they did not kill was a woman bearing a child on her back. And they let her live, that she might tell how terrible they were. And tales are now told of how terrible they were.

When the thunder spirits come, even the earth itself is stricken with terror. And stones, even those which lie on level ground, and not on any slope at all, roll in fear towards men.

Thus, the thunder comes with the south-westerly gales; there is a noise and crackling in the air, as of dry skins shaken, and the sky glows from time to time with the fire from their firestone. Great rocks, and everything which stands up high in the air, begin to glow.

When this happens, men use to take out a red dog, and cut its ear until the blood comes, and then lead the beast round about the house, letting the blood drip everywhere, for then the house will not take fire.

A red dog was the only thing they feared, those girls who were turned to thunder.

The Walking Stone

Yaqui

There was a beautiful young woman by the name of Sawali Wiikit, or, "Little Yellow Bird," who had lovely, long hair, and eyes as shining as a star. But there was one thing about her that was bad. She was disobedient, and she liked to walk about with her friends at night without asking permission of either her father or her mother. She would walk about until dawn and then come home to sleep.

One day, very early in the morning, Sawali Wiikit came into the house to sleep. But before she could lie down her mother spoke to her, "Listen to me, Sawali Wiikit, I don't want you to walk about like this either in the nighttime or in the daytime. I want to you to help me with the things of the household. It would be well for you to stop walking about day and night."

Sawali Wiikit did not reply, but she planned in her heart to continue on her midnight walks in the company of men. She slept, and again at night she left the house. She went to the home of another woman who always went with her. This girl's name was Maso Hubi'aria. She didn't walk about at night, but she would serve Sawali Wiikit pitahaya wine there in her house. That night they drank and became intoxicated. By dawn, Sawali Wiikit was quite drunk on pitahaya wine. When she arrived home, her mother and her father spoke to her.

Her father said, "If you are not going to stop all of this vice and begin to respect your parents, then you will do me the favor of going away. Go anywhere you please."

"Yes, my father, I will go."

"Wait a moment," he said, and he went out of the house. The young girl waited, and her father soon returned carrying a long, flexible branch. With him came a maestro from the church of Rahum.

The maestro said to the girl, "So you think it better to leave your mother and father forever?"

"Yes," replied Sawali Wiikit.

Then the maestro said to her father, "Punish your daughter so that she will always remember you." So, her father gave her three lashes. And he said, "Now you may go."

The maestro accompanied her out of Rahum to the north. Near a mesquite tree he said, "Here you may beg forgiveness of Dios for your sins and your disobedience. If Dios forgives you, you may return to your home."

"But I don't want to return."

"Well, then ask Dios for some penance."

So, she knelt and said, "Dios, I do not want to return. I would rather become a tree or a stone or an animal. I do not want to be a good woman."

She had no more than finished speaking when she was changed into a stone.

The maestro went back to Rahum and told what had happened. All of the young people were frightened and were very good to their parents thereafter.

The stone of Sawali Wiikit walked from there to Rahum, to Guamuchil, to Potam, and toward Torim. Sometimes people would put it on top of a mesquite tree, but the next day they would find it somewhere else. Once they found it near Lencho, and they carried it to Torim and put it in front of the church. But it was not there at dawn. It is said that lately it has been seen in the vicinity of Vicam. This is the story of Sawali Wiikit, the walking stone. It ends here.

Nûñ'yunu'wï, the Stone Man

Cherokee

This is what the old men told me when I was a boy.

Once when all the people of the settlement were out in the mountains on a great hunt, one man who had gone on ahead climbed to the top of a high ridge, and found a large river on the other side. While he was looking across, he saw an old man walking about on the opposite ridge, with a cane that seemed to be made of some bright, shining rock. The hunter watched and saw that every little while, the old man would point his cane in a certain direction, then draw it back and smell the end of it.

At last, he pointed it in the direction of the hunting camp on the other side of the mountain, and this time when he drew back the staff, he sniffed it several times as if it smelled very good, and then started along the ridge straight for the camp. He moved very slowly, with the help of the cane, until he reached the end of the ridge, when he threw the cane out into the air and it became a bridge of shining rock stretching across the river. After he had crossed over upon the bridge it became a cane again, and the old man picked it up and started over the mountain toward the camp.

The hunter was frightened, and felt sure that it meant mischief, so he hurried on down the mountain and took the shortest trail back to the camp to get there before the old man. When he got there and told his story the medicine-man said the old man was a wicked cannibal monster called Nûñ'yunu'wï, "Dressed in Stone," who lived in that part of the country, and was always going about the mountains looking for some hunter to kill and eat. It was very hard to escape from him, because his stick guided him like a dog, and it was nearly as hard to kill him, because his whole body was covered with a skin of solid rock. If he came, he would kill and eat them all, and there was only one way to save themselves. He could not bear to look upon a menstrual woman, and if they could find seven menstrual women to stand in the path as he came along the sight would kill him.

So, they asked among all the women, and found seven who were sick in that way, and with one of them it had just begun. By the order of the medicine-man they stripped themselves and stood along the path where the old man would come. Soon they heard Nûñ'yunu'wï coming through the woods, feeling his way with his stone cane. He came along the trail to where the first woman was standing, and as soon as he saw her, he started and cried out: "*Yu!* my grandchild; you are in a very bad state!"

He hurried past her, but in a moment, he met the next woman, and cried out again: "*Yu!* my child; you are in a terrible way," and hurried past her, but now he was vomiting blood. He hurried on and met the third and the fourth and the fifth woman, but with each one that he saw his step grew weaker until when he came to the last one, with whom the sickness had just begun, the blood poured from his mouth and he fell down on the trail.

Then the medicine-man drove seven sourwood stakes through his body and pinned him to the ground, and when night came, they piled great logs over him and set fire to them, and all the people gathered around to see.

165

Nûñ'yunu'wï was a great ada'wehï and knew many secrets, and now as the fire came close to him, he began to talk, and told them the medicine for all kinds of sickness. At midnight he began to sing, and sang the hunting songs for calling up the bear and the deer and all the animals of the woods and mountains. As the blaze grew hotter his voice sank low and lower, until at last when daylight came, the logs were a heap of white ashes and the voice was still.

Then the medicine-man told them to rake off the ashes, and where the body had lain, they found only a large lump of red wâ'dï paint and a magic u'lûñsû'ti stone. He kept the stone for himself, and calling the people around him he painted them, on face and breast, with the red wâ'dï, and whatever each person prayed for while the painting was being done-whether for hunting success, for working skill, or for a long life-that gift was his.

White Bead Woman

A Navaho Creation Myth

The Sun said to the two War Twins. "Go to your mother and get her to go to the west to the ocean. This is so I can see my wife. White Bead Woman, from now on." The Sun had asked her himself, but White Bead Woman had said, "I will be lonesome there all by myself, and I will become homesick." This is why the Sun said to the Twins, "I will give all my things, all you want, all my possessions, if you get her to go there. I have done many things for you; now repay me for my kindness. Go tell your mother to go to the west."

This is what the Sun said to his sons. The Sun had many wives besides her, but White Bead Woman was jealous. That is why she did not want to go. The Sun was not coming to see every day, but only once a week. The Twins went to see their mother, but still White Bead Woman did not want to go to the west, even then. All of the rest of the gods tried to help the Twins have their mother go to the west. Still, she refused to go.

There was one man that did not know all of this excitement was taking place. This god was very strong so everyone decided to let him try to make White Bead Woman go west. The gods said, "We will have him try." This god was

xaśč'éšžiní, the Black, Flint or Fire God. None of the
people had fire, only this xaśč'éšžiní, for he was the Fire
God. He would rub a stick that had been rubbed in some
rocks and make fire. This was a type of a match and this
was the first time and place matches were made. The idea
came from here for people to make matches today. All
around the home of Black God was coal burning, instead of
firewood.

The old man was told to go and tell White Bead Woman to
go west. He went to her and said, "How come all of your
children tell you to go west to your husband, but you still
don't want to go? Why?" He tried his best to try and make
her go, but she still would not leave her home. At last, he
got desperate and said, "If you don't want to go to the west,
all of the earth and gods shall be burned up." He got angrier
and angrier and finally took his weapon out to start the fire
(it was a rock torch). This fire was to start all over the
world and would be so bad that even the water would catch
on fire. Black God struck the two rocks together, or rather
ground them, and they began to smoke. After he had done
this only twice, the woman stopped him.

If he had done this for four times, everything on earth
would have burned up. After this she started to cry and put
her arms around the old man and said she would go to the
west forever. White Bead Woman gathered all of her
property in a white bead basket and prayed to Supreme
Sacred Wind for all of the animals and seed plants. The
seeds and plants prayed for fell into the basket and the
animals gathered outside of her hogan.

At this time White Bead Woman received another name,
Receive-Things-in-her-Hand, xāēlǎ kǎ eyá gī', because of
this. Some of the animals she put into her basket and some
who were left over had to walk. The cattle had been made

out of Mirage Quartz Rock by White Bead Woman. She took Mirage Quartz Rock powder and water and molded them into the right shape and size. When she placed them in water, they became alive.

They were told, "You will be dangerous and even your voices will be danger, but you will be used for good. You are to be used by the Earth People." She had it in her mind to do things this way. The Supreme Sacred Wind did not tell her to do this. These cattle were placed in baskets of white shell. When White Bead Woman traveled west, she took out a male, and female cattle and put them in the spring at Fierce Water Spring at Pasture Canyon. No others, not her sons or the Sun or Frog Man had any cattle. These cattle were for all the Earth People.

Besides the animals in the basket she placed inside seeds, nuts, berries and roots. Her basket was made out of shell and had a finish on top of it, just like the marriage basket. These baskets of all five colors are still in the ocean where they were left by White Bead Woman. Some of the animals were left over and could not be carried in the basket, so they followed her to the west. As she started to the west there was an earthquake. The earth at this time was still just like water underneath. When she started from her New Mexican home, White Bead Woman spent a night at Red Mesa, near where Tuba City, Arizona, is now.

While she was spending the night there with her animals, they moved around in a circle and would not settle down. White Bead Woman made three posts out of black rock. These are the rocks that are found near where Tuba City is now called Black Butte, another near Navaho Mountain called Wildcat Butte and one in Colorado called Black Post Butte. The mountain by the Gap, Arizona, was beautiful and in one long piece at this time. The animals were so numerous that they wore this mountain down by going over it so many times and that is why it looks like that today. Another part of it, to the southwest of Navaho Mountain, was worn down by their crossing over it so many times, too. The animals were thus enclosed by these mountains and the Little and Big Colorado Rivers.

After the animals became calm during the night, she went to the canyon where the water meets from the two great rivers. It was here at the junction of the Colorado Rivers that Salt Woman was created. She was created from the water washing back and forth against the rock or soil of a mountain. From the salty foam she was created—as if it were intercourse. Salt Woman was created long before White Bead Woman, and they were not related even by clan.

There is a story about Salt Woman at the junction of the Colorado Rivers where she was created. Near there is a hill which is of rocks shaped like a hogan. In the center of this is a hole which has water inside. This water never overflows the hole and two ladders reach up from this water to within three feet of the top. If this hole looks black there will be lots of rain. There were gods that came up with Salt Woman in a cane like the other gods in New Mexico. There is a salt trail which has a marker to show where it is. Here is the hole which the Hopi claim as theirs. (The hole referred to is perhaps the one visited by the Hopi in their quest for salt. Intercourse is simulated with the hole and gifts left for the Salt Woman.

There is a jackass hoof print made by some of the Salt Woman's animals as she drove them out of the hole to the west side of Shadow Mountain. She became warm and threw the sweat from her forehead, and it made the soil salty there. She continued up the Little Colorado Canyon and left a finger mark there upon the wall. When everything is good upon the earth, the mark is new; if it is old, then things are evil in the world. It was there at the junction of the rivers that Salt Woman and White Bead Woman met. Salt Woman drove on to Shadow Mountain while White Bead Woman later drove on to the west.

Salt Woman went on to Winslow, Holbrook, Salt or'áši̧h, Arizona. There is a lake or reservoir that people can get salt from. Salt Woman now lives there. After you get salt from the junction or the Salt Lake, should you look back or jiggle the load or try to adjust the pack, it will become heavier and heavier. It will also become heavier as you continue to walk on.

White Bead Woman sat there by the bank and then stepped back from the water. She then made a fire and prepared to stay the night. There is a gap down in the canyon where this happened. As she sat there, there appeared a fine young man out of the water called Sea Horse. This man looked like a horse, yet was a man. She spent a night with this man upon ground which was solid or hard. The next morning White Bead Woman had blood coming from her vagina, and this was the first period or menstruation in the world. The animals outside of her basket were later lost because of this infidelity. She left there as a gift to this man, salt, shell, turquoise, jet, white bead, oyster shell and red shell. These things are still there to this day. These gifts were all for this man.

After she had done this, she urinated into the Little Colorado and that is why it is now red as it runs into the Big Colorado. The next morning, she went back to the top of the mountain where she had left all of her animals. As she got to the top of the mountain, she found all of her animals gone. On the west of Cedar Ridge is a mountain that was originally the escaped wild sheep from the herds of White Bead Woman. All of the wild sheep and most of the animals who escaped later turned into mountains. All of these animals that did not turn into mountains went into the Kaibab Forest and are still there. That is the reason there are so many game animals there now.

Near the joining of the two rivers is another gap where White Bead Woman went across with the few animals left in the basket. (There were still left the deer, antelope, all of the meat animals, turquoise, berries, corn, squash, etc.) She ate some of the corn seeds for her lunch on the way to the west. She went on to Mesa Verde and to ch·ōsgí. There is a pattern of the Sun there—a sand painting. It is still there and people pray to this Sun and no one can go there unless he has the right prayer.

It is important because White Bead Woman made the Sun pattern. It was made on a rock and planted near there was a plant called Black Medicine, 'aze·'łižin, and a plant called Big or Large Medicine, 'aze·'coh. These two medicines are used in many ways and for many things. She brought the plants with her from the east. If anything goes wrong on the earth, the pattern looks old, and if everything is well, the pattern looks new. The location of the pattern is not known. She planted oak trees further on. Near these she piled some rocks for a marker to tell the trail which she called Pile-of-Rocks.

White Bead Woman continued on to Hopi Towers and on to Gray Mountain and on to the south side of Grand Canyon. She went right on until she arrived at the sea near the highest mountain in California, Mount Whitney. All of the people gathered around her when she arrived. All of the gods living near this area gathered and some even came from the home of White Bead Woman to the east. On top of this mountain was a hogan. If you look there now, it is still there. If you should look at this hogan when things are going bad, then it will look old. If it looks new, then affairs in the world are going to be good.

There are many things on the top of this mountain such as turquoise, flints, black shining dirt, pollen, white bead, horses of stone and many other things. All things that the medicine men made use of then and now can be found there. One of the gods picked up a boy and girl when they came from the east. He took them so that these children could be taught all the songs of the gods before they left the earth. White Bead Woman knew all of the songs which the rest of the gods did not. These children were to learn everything from her.

The gods did not have soapweed in the west where they were, so they had a talk to decide what to use for soap in the ceremonies. The War Twins, meanwhile, did not know there was going to be a sing for these children in order to teach them all of the sacred things the White Bead Woman knew. In fact, they did not even know that the children had been taken to the west. The gods finally decided to bury jet, flint, white bead, oyster shell and turquoise so that a plant of soap would grow. They planted these things in the evening and the sing was held over the boy and girl all during the night.

The sing was held because these children had learned all from the White Bead Woman. They now could instruct the rest of the people while White Bead Woman was gone to the west. The dance was held now and the gods danced over the side of these seed materials. These seeds soon began to grow. In the morning they dug up the yucca and were now ready to make soap. During the ceremony they put plants underneath a basket which were pinyon, cedar, evergreen, fir, spruce and kinds of plants, but no pine. The basket was made of white bead like before and was about the size of a marriage basket.

At the time of the sing over the children the War Twins did not know that it was taking place, but they heard a rumor about it. The First Twin started off with a friend, God-Water-Carrier. The First Twin had gone to this friend and told him to go on a journey with him. This friend lived at White-Water-Fall. As they left on their trip it started to rain. They were in this rain all the way down to California. When they got there, the rain went on past the hogan and they went inside.

Inside the hogan, the First Twin asked his mother. "Why didn't you tell me you were here and that this ceremony was going on? Am I the wrong kind of a god? Why didn't you notify me? Aren't I entitled to be notified?" White Bead Woman answered her son saying, "I know you have nothing to do or say about what is going on out here. That is why we did not notify you."

Then the Twin said. "Have these children learned all the power that they are going to learn?" These children were still Earth People and not yet gods. "Is there any more for them to learn?" White Bead Woman said, "No, this is why we have picked these children. The people did not learn all of my power. I am going away with all the power, but now all of your Earth People will know everything." The Twins were gods and there were also many gods all over the world. The War Gods and the other gods at times were bad, disobedient, and not right. That is why she was "so stingy" with her knowledge. No one knew as much as she did about the ways of the world.

After White Bead Woman had answered her son, he said, "It is fine that these children know all and have all the power." He asked another question, "Did they learn the Good Way Song? Did they learn all the songs of the Five Night Sings? Did they learn the War Songs? Did they learn the Yeibache Songs? Did they learn all the other songs?" She answered saying, "It is all complete. All of these things have been learned. Now I do not have to worry about anything." They had all the power gained from knowing these things for they were not gods, but humans. That night the people finished the singing. In the morning the gods decided to send the children back with the Navaho—after they were to create them.

White Bead Woman in the morning took dirt from her chest and made the figures of two people. From her back she took more dirt and molded two more figures. From her right palm she molded two more figures. From the left palm she took dirt and once again molded two small figures. From the right foot dirt was taken and from the left more dirt and molded into figures. At last, there were twelve small figures of humans—half of the figures women and half men. Each time White Bead Woman made the figures, she took her fingernail paring and the grease from her body along with the dirt to mold them. That is the reason we get so dirty. If she had not made Navahos from fingernail paring, this would not have happened. This is the reason why the Navaho get so dirty, in particular.

It is the belief of the Navaho that dirt comes from the food which we eat. As we eat dirty things or salty foods especially, this dirt comes from the inside of the body from the things we eat. Because of this, the Navaho take sweat baths to make these wastes come from the pores. This is the reason the Navaho use the sweat bath so much, in order to get rid of the body wastes. When other people take a hot bath, if not a Navaho, it is for the same purpose.

The people who were created were Navaho. The dirt had been taken and molded into figures like us, but very tiny. All of them were laid on the ground with a Never-Been-Shot-Buckskin put over the top and with one on the bottom. These figures were prayed and sung over by the White Bead Woman, Talking God and all of the other gods. After this was done, these small figures came to life and grew to full size. These people were to be called Created-Navaho, diné 'alya·ígí. These twelve people were then sent along with the two children to the east where the gods had been in the beginning.

After all this had happened, White Bead Woman continued to the west. From here are two stories—one to the west and one coming back to the east. We shall now follow the story to the west. White Bead Woman started off, and the gods went to places where they were to stay forever. Some of the gods went into the earth, some into the heavens, some into the mountains and some into the water. These gods became settled and said, "From now on no person shall see us again."

On the other side of the Gap there is a wall where there is a picture of a Yeibache with a white face and feathers. It if shows up good to the eye and is easily seen, there will be rain. If not, then there will be no rain. This represents the Talking God, Yeibache. He has twelve feathers on his head. When there is a Yeibache Dance, the others in the dance will have two feathers, and the last dancer has twelve turkey feathers and is Calling God. This last man is the clown of the dance and picks up anything that falls from the other dancers. He can do this for he is the funny man.

Calling God is a clown while Talking God is always taking care of everyone.

The gods made the promise that they would never be seen or talked to by the Earth People. People were never to see the gods or angels again. "You will see us, but we will be flowers, grass, plants, trees, rocks, earth, lightning and everything upon the earth. These will show you that we are still with you." All the Navaho, therefore, pray to all of these for they *represent* the gods themselves *and are not the gods*. This was told to the people at this time. When it rains and there is nothing showing on the ground, plants and flowers appear. These are the gods themselves. Anything that grows represents the gods. Birds, stars, clouds, rain are all gods.

Some of the gods went back to Black Belt Mountain, sísnajïni, and some went to the mountain by Crown Point Mountain, some to the other six mountains, and still lesser gods into the other mountains of the earth. Any place where there are black stripes on the earth is found represents Talking God. Water running out of the earth also represents him. Some of the gods went into all kinds of trees. (F. G. would not tell the names of the gods and where they went for, he felt he would lose his power as a medicine man. A man who was not a medicine man would have no power to lose and thus could tell.) These trees move and act as if they were alive. After all this had happened, all of the gods left and said. "We will never see each other again."

After the Twin had finished talking to his mother, he did not stay for the sing. He went back to his home at Reversible Mountain and he and his brother went towards Williams, over where Prescott Copper Mine is now, to change into rocks. There are two rocks that look like the Twins at this place now. The souls (spirits) of the Twins are still in these rocks. They have all their power there, and can hear the prayers of the Earth People. If the world changes, they will come back to life and destroy all the evil—like before. The Twins got their power from the Sun and will keep it until more troubles come upon the earth.

Should the world change, the Twins, White Bead Woman and all of the other gods will return to earth. All of the gods taught the Twin certain powers to kill all of the evil upon the earth. The gods had equal power, but all in different ways. White Bead Woman was taught in the same way as the Twins were later. The reason the War Twins won the wars with their enemies is the same reason the United States always wins their wars—the War Twins are on the good side. If the Navaho were with the Russians or Germans, they would have been the ones who would win the wars. The Navaho speech was used in the Pacific and the people learned the Navaho had the power, and that is why they were used to help the allies.

White Bead Woman went out to the Sun's house that was in the sea. Some medicine men say she traveled on foot to the west, but she is a god and does not travel in this way. The house of the Sun was sitting on the ocean, but was not an island. Sometimes people see it, but not all of the time. It was made of turquoise, white bead, jet and oyster shell. White Bead Woman looked at the house and blew a rainbow spectrum to the house. She got on it and rode to the house on the ocean. Nowadays we have boats like this house according to what the house of the Sun did. Ships have rooms, beds and all the things that the house of the Sun had. The Sun's house is like a submarine and sinks sometimes into the sea and that is why you cannot see it. White Bead Woman reached the Sun's house in the evening.

The Sun was glad to see her and he laughed and kissed her because of his happiness. Everything was in the house that she needed. The house was made as follows: The floor of the middle room was made of oyster shell polished like marble. The walls were also of oyster shell. To the east room the floor and walls were of polished white bead. To the south were floors and walls of turquoise. To the west there was again a room of oyster shell. In the last room, to the north, were black jet walls and floor. This house was like the Sun's house to the east.

This house also had clouds on all of the walls. In the middle room was a white male and female cloud on the wall. To the south was a blue male and female cloud. To the west was a yellow male and female cloud. Upon the north wall was a black male and female cloud. In this house were also seen the mortar and pestle in the floor and the many flints on the walls. After White Bead Woman had been there four days, she began getting old age (about 400 years old). If White Bead Woman had not gotten old at this time, it would not have been possible for old age to come about now.

After these four days had passed, she went into the east room, and when she came out, she was younger. After going into each of the rooms and finally coming out of the last one to the north, she was again a young girl. Even today she gets very old every four years, and she has to go through this procedure. Because of the four rooms, she will get young every four years, too. First Man and First Woman live at the east in the Sun's house, and they, too, get old every four years. They, too must do the same as the White Bead Woman.

All the other gods became old every twelve years, and when this happens, they all come together. There is a meeting place which is at another Black Mountain on the other side of Holbrook called Woodruff Buttes or tˣo·žį'xʷi·zo. These gods have a meeting there every night to talk matters over. Anyone who wants to, can hear these gods. These gods, unlike the others talked about, become young every twelve years. They, too, have a house so that when they get old, they can go through it and become young again.

The Sun also gets old like the other gods and has to go through his house so that he will get young again. White Bead Woman spent most of her time in the middle or center room. It was at this time that she got the name of Changing Woman, or Woman-Who-Changes. The house to the east is made the same as the one to the west. The Sun's other wife lives there.

The story now continues on to the east from Mount Whitney with the fourteen people. The people came out towards their ancient lands with the male and female bear, male and female big snake, male and female thunder bird, male and female wind, male and female mountain lion and the male and female wolf. The job of these animals was to protect the people from any evil or harm. They were pets to the people. These people were trying to make pets or dogs out of the wolves as they traveled along.

When they came to Williams, they met some Arrow People in human form. They fought with these Arrow People and when the fourteen people were about to be beaten, they turned to the bears and asked for help from them. The bears began to fight and to kill all of the enemy. Victorious, the people continued on to the west of San Francisco Peaks. There they found a spring where there are two mountains together. This place was called Where-They-Spent-a-Night-with-the-Bears.

There are two stories here which come out from this story. One goes to the Leupp and the other goes through Tuba City, Arizona. The one that goes along the Loop is a male story and the one through Tuba is a female story. There is a different version of each story according to the direction. There is a flat mountain on the end of San Francisco Peaks. This mountain is Chipped Off Mountain or ził k'élkal. The lions were always behind, and the people finally left them there. The two mountain lions wore out their paws and they were told, "That is where you are going to stay from this time on. You will be used in the future times by the Earth People. Your skin will be quivers, your claws shall become necklaces and your fat shall be used for medicine."

The people continued along the top of the mountains and one person was carrying the big snake. The man got tired and let the big snake go on the ground. This snake escaped and it is still living in the lava rock, but no one has seen it. "Sometimes he will be seen in the future time," it was said. The people also told the male big snake he would be used in the future. It was the male snake that was left there and the female was carried on. If people do not have corn pollen, it can be shaken off of a big snake (or bear, thunder, tornado or wind). This was to be the purpose of big snake and this pollen was to be used in the future time. Some medicine men use this type of pollen for certain rites. The claws of the wolf and mountain lion are used in the same ways.

The travelers went on and crossed at Tuba Wash, near the Colorado River and went across Cameron. Lava Rock by Cameron shows the place they crossed the Colorado River. The people got a drink at the spring, Black Spring, on the other side of Cameron and went on to Shadow Mountain. Long ago there used to be tiny dogs barking in that spring. (F. G. does not know why.) All the people decided to spend a night at Shadow Mountain. They had come to Willow Springs after Shadow Mountain. At the game corral at Shadow Mountain there is a spring called Hard-Ground-Around-the-Spring or tˣóbe·xʷi·sgáń.

They went to Willow Springs to the north side of Tuba City and then on to the northeast of the Hopi Reservation at Moenkopi. They followed along where the highway to Tuba is now towards White Mesa. From White Mesa they went to a spring on the east side called Covered-up-Spring or tˣók'i·šže'é. They continued on to Red Lake and then to Cow Springs and towards Shonto.

While they were going towards Cow Springs, two captured Arrow children began playing. The children were eating wild onions and plants as they went through this country, and this is why they were behind. At Shonto, the wanderers waited for the two children to catch up with them. The travelers said. "We will wait. We have two children to come." One person went back to get the two children. He could not find them and came back and told the people they were gone. He looked for tracks and found some leading towards Red Lake.

At the road to Red Lake there is a hump along a flat area. When the man went around this hump, he saw two children going to Red Lake and so he ran after them. He came around the point of the hill and got into the open and saw the children going into the rocks. These two children became the Elephant's Feet. The first one was the boy and the next one was the girl. The boy was from the Water-Coming-Together-Clan. The girl was of the Edge-Water-Clan. All of the leaders or heads of the clans carried canes as they walked along.

There is another story which also tells of the travels of the fourteen. The White Bead Woman made the different clans when the people were first made. They were given their names by her. The first two people to be made were called Along-the-Mountain-Clan. Their pet was to be the male and female mountain lion. This is the reason why the Navahos of this clan are heavy set and have stub noses. This clan had a turquoise cane which they carried with them.

The people created from the back of White Bead Woman were called the Mud Clan, having as a mascot a male and female bear with the leader carrying a white bead cane. The people created from the left hand of White Bead Woman became the Near-the-Water-Clan, having a pet male and female big snake and carrying a cane made out of dark oyster shell. The people from the right hand of White Bead Woman were called the Bitter-Water-Clan with a pet of a male and female thunder bird and carrying a jet cane. The people from the left foot were called Many-Goats-Clan with a pet male and female wind god and carrying a cane out of red stone, célčí·' (The informant's first statement was that these people of the left foot carried *no* cane. On later discussion the sentence was changed as above. The reasoning behind this is not known for certain, but in all the available versions of the Creation Myths, there are twelve people created, with but *four* leaders and *four* canes.)

The people created from White Bead Woman's right foot were called the Black-Sheep-Clan having a pet male and female wolf. These people had a cane of different kind of oyster shell called very white oyster shell. On the way back to the original land of the Navaho there was much water found along the way. As the different people set out from the White Bead Woman, they took along their pets with them.

They met and captured some Arrow People, ka·' dine'é, as has been explained before, and killed the rest. The clan that did this was the Bitter-Water-Clan. The two posts or Elephant's Feet were a boy and a girl from the Arrow People. It was not the boy or girl who had received all of the power that got lost, but these captured Arrow People that turned into rocks. The boy and girl were trying to escape and go back home to their own people. The home of some of the gods was at Shadow Mountain. They were to have had a Fire Dance when they arrived at night.

There are two stories here; one is as correct as the other. One goes like this: Near this mountain there is a gully with rocks all around it for it was an antelope corral. Later it changed into a mountain. This is where the god's caught antelope for meat. There were four ways to get into the corral from the four directions. The other story is that this mountain is a hogan. Gods now have their home in Shadow Mountain.

There are trees on top of Shadow Mountain where the gods dried meat. There is also a flat rock to dry meat upon at Shadow Mountain, so the story goes. There are, then, the two stories: One which tells about the hogan and the Fire Dance, and the other about the catching of the antelope by these people. There is also a rope that changed into a rock there. The head man sat inside of the hogan gathering power to round the antelope up. When the people went hunting the heads of the deer and the buckskins were put on the people, and they were thus disguised and were able to kill the animals. The power is lost to man to gather antelope and deer now as it was done in the old days.

The Snake Man

Cherokee

Two hunters, both for some reason under a tabu against the meat of a squirrel or turkey, had gone into the woods together. When evening came, they found a good camping place and lighted a fire to prepare their supper. One of them had killed several squirrels during the day, and now got ready to broil them over the fire. His companion warned him that if he broke the tabu and ate squirrel meat he would become a snake, but the other laughed and said that was only a conjurer's story. He went on with his preparation, and when the squirrels were roasted made his supper of them and then lay down beside the fire to sleep.

Late that night his companion was aroused by groaning, and on looking around he found the other lying on the ground rolling and twisting in agony, and with the lower part of his body already changed to the body and tail of a large water snake. The man was still able to speak and called loudly for help, but his companion could do nothing, but only sit by and try to comfort him while he watched the arms sink into the body and the skin take on a scaly change that mounted gradually toward the neck, until at last even the head was a serpent's head and the great snake crawled away from the fire and down the bank into the river.

The Spirit Fox

Yaqui

An Indian lived in the region of the hill west of Bacum. This man's name was Ba'ayoeria. Alone, he and his woman lived. They had neighbors a little distance away to the north, and others farther away to the south. Ba'ayoeria was not a hunter. He lived from collecting roots for medicines and edible roots. Also, he collected blossoms from trees for use in tanning hides and others for medicines. He would load them in some coyote or fox hide sacks, or wildcat skin sacks. Then he would set out, carrying various sacks full of roots and flowers, crossing the hills and higher mountains to the edge of the sea. All these things he would exchange for dried fish, clams, oysters, and salt--all of these for his woman, and for his neighbors who brought him skins in exchange for salt, fish and oysters. In this way, he was living.

One day when Ba'ayoeria traveled in search of roots, a fox passed in front of him and stopped, gazing at him. Ba'ayoeria went on his way, looking back now and again at the fox who was still watching him.

The same thing happened the second day. On the third day, at the same place, the fox came out and spoke, saying, "Listen to me, Ba'ayoeria. This is a true thing. I am your friend. I am not really a fox, but I asked permission to come here with you because I am looking at a great danger that will come to you and I want to save you. This night an individual is coming with intentions to kill you. Your woman is having amorous relations with this man and they are agreed upon killing you. For some time, they have been playing treasonously with you. Tonight, don't lie down in your bed in the place where you are accustomed to sleep. Put your wife there where you usually sleep because she has told the man, 'Thus you may kill him as he sleeps and we will live together without danger from Ba'ayoeria.' Thus, your wife spoke."

All of this, the fox told to Ba'ayoeria who then asked, "Who are you?"

"I am the soul of that lost body you buried near Buram Teopo. In gratitude for your having buried my body, I, today, advise you."

"Good, then, little fox," said the Indian.

The fox disappeared into the thicket and the man returned to his hut, and to his woman. That evening, after supper they chatted awhile. The two appeared to be contented, nothing could be seen, not a bad word or a bad look. The two conversed until bedtime came.

And when it came time to lie down, the man said to the wife, "Let us change places. You sleep in my place, and I in yours."

The woman took her head in her hands, and he asked, "Why do you appear so sad?"

"I don't know what happened to me," replied the woman.

"Come, then, lie down in my place and you will feel better," he said. The woman lay down and pretended to sleep.

But Ba'ayoeria did not sleep. Late at night the traitor came quietly. He moved up to the bed where the woman lay, thinking it was Ba'ayoeria. He lifted his arm and gave a great stab with his sharp, wooden lance. Ba'ayoeria arose, threw himself on the man and overcame him. He tied him firmly with ropes and waited for the dawn to come. In the morning he buried his woman.

He took the assassin to Bacum. There, the man was punished with lashes until blood gushed from between his shoulder-blades. From these lashes he died two days later.

Ba'ayoeria married another young girl, and continued his work of trading roots and flowers.

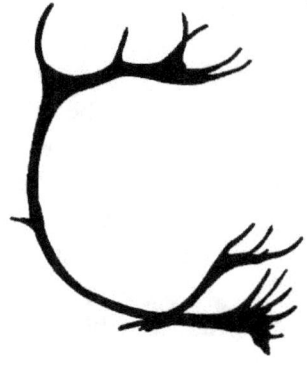

The Snake Boy

Cherokee

There was a boy who used to go bird hunting every day, and all the birds he brought home he gave to his grandmother, who was very fond of him. This made the rest of the family jealous, and they treated him in such fashion that at last one day he told his grandmother he would leave them all, but that she must not grieve for him.

Next morning, he refused to eat any breakfast, but went off hungry to the woods and was gone all day. In the evening he returned, bringing with him a pair of deer horns, and went directly to the hothouse (âsï), where his grandmother was waiting for him. He told the old woman he must be alone that night, so she got up and went into the house where the others were.

At early daybreak she came again to the hothouse and looked in, and there she saw an immense uktena that filled the âsï, with horns on its head, but still with two human legs instead of a snake tail. It was all that was left of her boy. He spoke to her and told her to leave him, and she went away again from the door.

When the sun was well up, the uktena began slowly to crawl out, but it was full noon before it was all out of the âsï. It made a terrible hissing noise as it came out, and all the people ran from it. It crawled on through the settlement, leaving a broad trail in the ground behind it, until it came to a deep bend in the river, where it plunged in and went under the water.

The grandmother grieved much for her boy, until the others of the family got angry and told her that as she thought so much of him, she ought to go and stay with him. So, she left them and went along the trail made by the uktena to the river and walked directly into the water and disappeared.

Once after that, a man fishing near the place saw her sitting on a large rock in the river, looking just as she had always looked, but as soon as she caught sight of him, she jumped into the water and was gone.

More Tales of the Native American Indians

The Mounds and The Constant Fire: The Old Sacred Things

Cherokee

Some, say that the mounds were built by another people. Others say they were built by the ancestors of the old Ani'-Kïtu'hwagï for townhouse foundations, so that the townhouses would be safe when freshets came. The townhouse was always built on the level bottom lands by the river in order that the people might have smooth ground for their dances and ballplays and might be able to go down to water during the dance.

When they were ready to build the mound, they began by laying a circle of stones on the surface of the ground. Next, they made a fire in the center of the circle and put near it the body of some prominent chief or priest who had lately died--some say seven chief men from the different clans--together with an Ulûñsû'tï stone, an uktena scale or horn, a feather from the right wing of an eagle or great tlä'nuwä, which lived in those days, and beads of seven colors, red, white, black, blue, purple, yellow, and gray-blue. The priest then conjured all these with disease, so that, if ever an enemy invaded the country, even though he should burn and destroy the town and the townhouse, he would never live to return home.

The mound was then built up with earth, which the women brought in baskets, and as they piled it above the stones, the bodies of their great men, and the sacred things, they left an open place at the fire in the center and let down a hollow cedar trunk, with the bark on, which fitted around the fire and protected it from the earth. This cedar log was cut long enough to reach nearly to the surface inside the townhouse when everything was done. The earth was piled up around it, and the whole mound was finished off smoothly, and then the townhouse was built upon it. One man, called the fire keeper, stayed always in the townhouse to feed and tend the fire. When there was to be a dance or a council, he pushed long stalks of the *ihyâ'ga* weed, which some call *atsil'-sûn'tï*, "the fire maker" (*Erigeron canadense*, or fleabane), down through the opening in the cedar log to the fire at the bottom. He left the ends of the stalks sticking out and piled lichens and punk around, after which he prayed, and as he prayed the fire climbed up along the stalks until it caught the punk. Then he put on wood, and by the time the dancers were ready there was a large fire blazing in the townhouse. After the dance he covered the hole over again with ashes, but the fire was always smoldering below. Just before the Green-corn dance, in the old times, every fire in the settlement was extinguished and all the people came and got new fire from the townhouse. This was called atsi'la gälûñkw`ti'yu "the honored or sacred fire." Sometimes when the fire in a house went out, the woman came to the fire keeper, who made a new fire by rubbing an ihyâ'ga stalk against the under side of a hard dry fungus that grows upon locust trees.

Some say this everlasting fire was only in the larger mounds at Nïkwäsï', Kïtu'hwa, and a few other towns, and that when the new fire was thus drawn up for the Green-corn dance it was distributed from them to the other settlements. The fire burns yet at the bottom of these great mounds, and when the Cherokee soldiers were camped near

Kïtu'hwa during the civil war they saw smoke still rising from the mound.

The Cherokee once had a wooden box, nearly square and wrapped up in buckskin, in which they kept the most sacred things of their old religion. Upon every important expedition two priests carried it in turn and watched over it in camp so that nothing could come near to disturb it. The Delawares captured it more than a hundred years ago, and after that the old religion was neglected and trouble came to the Nation. They had also a great peace pipe, carved from white stone, with seven stem-holes, so that seven men could sit around and smoke from it at once at their peace councils. In the old town of Keowee they had a drum of stone, cut in the shape of a turtle, which was hung up inside the townhouse and used at all the town dances. The other towns of the Lower Cherokee used to borrow it, too, for their own dances.

All the old things are gone now and the Indians are different.

Hemp-carrier

Cherokee

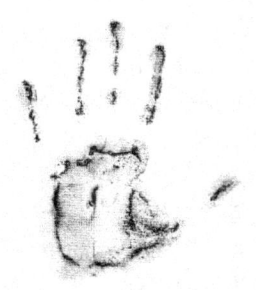

On the southern slope of the ridge, along the trail from Robbinsville to Valley River, in Cherokee county, North Carolina, are the remains of a number of stone cairns. The piles are leveled now, but thirty years ago the stones were still heaped up into pyramids, to which every Cherokee who passed added a stone. According to the tradition these piles marked the graves of a number of women and children of the tribe who were surprised and killed on the spot by a raiding party of the Iroquois shortly before the final peace between the two Nations. As soon as the news was brought to the settlements on Hiwassee and Cheowa a party was made under Tâle'tanigi'skï, "Hemp-carrier," to follow and take vengeance on the enemy. Among others of the party was the father of the noted chief Tsunu'lähûñ'skï, or Junaluska, who (Junaluska) died on Cheowa about 1855.

For days they followed the trail of the Iroquois across the Great Smoky mountains, through forests and over rivers, until they finally tracked them to their very town in the far northern Seneca country. On the way they met another war party headed for the south, and the Cherokee killed them all and took their scalps. When they came near the Seneca town it was almost night, and they heard shouts in the townhouse, where the women were dancing over the fresh Cherokee scalps. The avengers hid themselves near the spring, and as the dancers came down to drink the Cherokee silently killed one and another until they had counted as many scalps as had been taken on Cheowa, and still the dancers in the townhouse never thought that enemies were near. Then said the Cherokee leader, "We have covered the scalps of our women and children. Shall we go home now like cowards, or shall we raise the war whoop and let the Seneca know that we are men?" "Let them come, if they will," said his men; and they raised the scalp yell of the Cherokee. At once there was an answering shout from the townhouse, and the dance came to a sudden stop. The Seneca warriors swarmed out with ready gun and hatchet, but the nimble Cherokee were off and away. There was a hot pursuit in the darkness, but the Cherokee knew the trails and were light and active runners, and managed to get away with the loss of only a single man. The rest got home safely, and the people were so well pleased with Hemp-carrier's bravery and success that they gave him seven wives.

When Babies Are Born: The Wren and The Cricket

Cherokee

The little Wren is the messenger of the birds, and pries into everything. She gets up early in the morning and goes round to every house in the settlement to get news for the bird council. When a new baby is born, she finds out whether it is a boy or girl and reports to the council. If it is a boy the birds sing in mournful chorus: "Alas! the whistle of the arrow! my shins will burn," because the birds know that when the boy grows older, he will hunt them with his blowgun and arrows and roast them on a stick.

But if the baby is a girl, they are glad and sing: "Thanks! the sound of the pestle! At her home I shall surely be able to scratch where she sweeps," because they know that after a while, they will be able to pick up stray grains where she beats the corn into meal.

When the Cricket bears that a girl is born, it also is glad, and says, "Thanks, I shall sing in the house where she lives. "But if it is a boy the Cricket laments: "Alas! He will shoot me! He will shoot me! He will shoot me!" because boys make little bows to shoot crickets and grasshoppers.

When inquiring as to the sex of the new arrival the Cherokee asks, "Is it a bow or a (meal) sifter?" or, "Is it ballsticks or bread?"

About the Author

Thanks for choosing this book, if you enjoyed it, please leave positive feedback.

G.W. Mullins is an Author, Photographer, and Entrepreneur of Native American / Cherokee descent. He has been a published author for over 11 years. His writing has focused on the paranormal and Native American studies.

Mullins has released several books on the history/stories/fables of the Native American Indians. Among his books are the extremely successful "Star People, Sky Gods and Other Tales of the Native American Indians," "Story Teller An Anthology Of Folklore From The Native American Indians," "The Native American Story Book - Stories Of The American Indians For Children Volumes 1-5," "The Native American Cookbook," and "Walking With Spirits Native American Myths, Legends, And Folklore Volumes 1 Thru 6."

He has released the complete series of his Sci/fi Fantasy books "From The Dead Of Night," including the Best-Selling titles – "Daniel Is Waiting" and "Daniel Returns."

His most recent work includes the series "Rise Of The Snow Queen featuring Book One The Polar Bear King" and "Book Two War Of The Witches." Mullins' latest releases include two young adult fantasy series, "Rise of the Darklighter Book One: Dark Awakening" and the "Dream Walker" Book Series featuring "Enter the Sandman" & "Wide Awake In Dream Land." Among his other releases are "Messages from The Other Side" (a nonfiction book about communication with the dead), and the soon to be released "Convergence" (a post-apocalyptic book multi-series event coming in winter 2022).

For further information, on the writing, visit G.W. Mullins' web site at http://gwmullins.wix.com/books.

Also Available From G.W. Mullins

Daniel Awakens A Ghost Story Begins– From The Dead
Of Night Prequel

Daniel Is Waiting A Ghost Story – From The Dead Of
Night Book One

Daniel Returns A Ghost Story - From The Dead Of Night
Book Two

Daniel's Fate – A Ghost Story Ends From The Dead Of
Night Book Four

Rise Of The Snow Queen Book One The Polar Bear King

Messages From The Other Side Stories of the Dead, Their
Communication, and Unfinished Business

Vengeance

Mysteries Of The Unseen World – Ghost. Hauntings and
The Unexplained

Haunted America Stories Of Ghost, Hauntings And The
Unexplained

Timeless – A Paranormal Romance Murder Mystery

Star People, Sky Gods, And Other Tales Of The Native
American Indians

More Star People, Sky Gods, And Other Paranormal Tales
Of The Native American Indians

Coyote Tales Of The Native American Indians

Aliens, Gods, and Other Paranormal Native American Tales

Bear Tales Of The Native American Indians

Walking With Spirits Native American Myths, Legends,
And Folklore Volumes One Thru Six

The Native American Cookbook

Native American Cooking - An Indian Cookbook With
Legends And Folklore

The Native American Story Book - Stories Of The
American Indians For Children Volumes One Thru Five

The Best Native American Stories For Children

Cherokee A Collection of American Indian Legends,
Stories And Fables

Creation Myths - Tales Of The Native American Indians

Strange Tales Of The Native American Indians

Spirit Quest - Stories Of The Native American Indians

Animal Tales Of The Native American Indians

Medicine Man - Shamanism, Natural Healing, Remedies
And Stories Of The Native American Indians

Native American Legends: Stories Of The Hopi Indians
Volumes One and Two

Totem Animals Of The Native Americans

The Best Native American Myths, Legends And Folklore
Volumes One Thru Three

Ghosts, Spirits And The Afterlife In Native American
Indian Mythology And Folklore

War Song: Tales Of The Native American Indians

Origin Tales Of The Native American Indians

Animal Tales Of The Native American Indians Vol. 2

www.ingramcontent.com/pod-product-compliance
Lightning Source LLC
Chambersburg PA
CBHW071325120626
46546CB00002B/452